DATE DUE

MR 26 '93	FE 23 '98		
OC 8 '93			
DE 17 '93	OC 22 '98		
OC 21 '94	AP 26 '99		
DE 23 '94	AP 26 '99		
NY 19 '95	NV 17 '99		
	NO 16 '99		
	JE 10 '00		
JE 1 '95	DE 5 '01		
OC 27 '95	DE 12 '01		
DE 1 '95	NV 22 '02		
DE 22 '95	NO '03		
NV 11 '96	DE 7 '04		
DE 16 '96	DE 16 '06		
NV 25 '97	AP 9 '07		
NOV 7 '07			

DEMCO 38-296

Emergency Department

Hennepin County Medical Cent
701 P
Minneapolis, Mn 554
347-3

#128

ASSAULT

What is an assault?

An assault is when one person physically hurts, or attempts to hurt another person.

What is domestic assault?

This is when the victim is in, or has been in, a relationship with the person who hurt them.

Any type of assault is a crime.

If someone assaulted you, you were the victim of a crime. How serious the crime was depends upon the injuries you received.

Simple assault (also called fifth degree assault) is a misdemeanor. Injuries received in a simple assault may include:

- bruises
- swelling
- cuts

Serious assault (also called first, second or third degree assault) is a felony. Injuries received in a serious assault ma
include:

- broken bones
- temporary or perma
  part of your body
- temporary or perma
  of your organs (su
  loss of an eye)
- temporary, but ser
  stitches in your
  from coat hangers
- injury from a wea
  stabbed, or cut w
- threat of injury
  injured)

—01

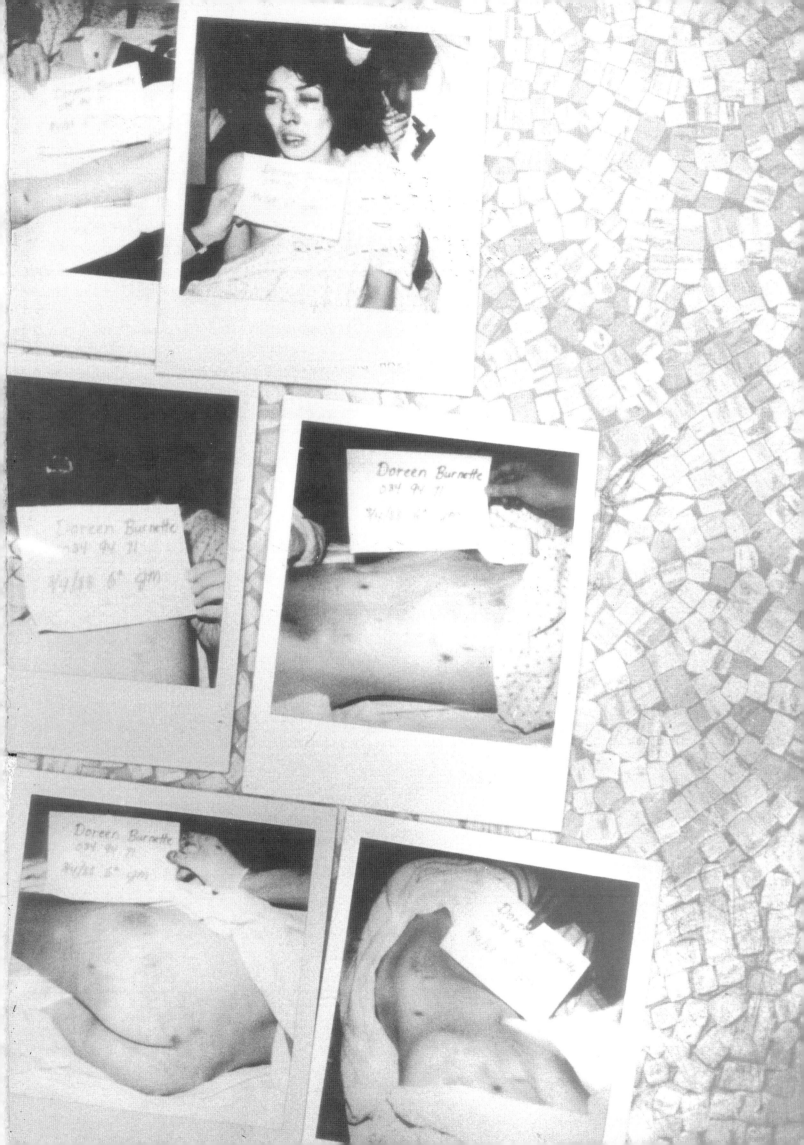

This book is about the dark side of family life.

Domestic violence did not threaten my childhood. Nor did it intrude into my world until ten years ago, when, on an assignment for a magazine, I saw a man hit his wife. I was unprepared for his violence—it shattered the belief I'd been raised with that home is a refuge from the chaos of life.

That experience changed my life as a photographer. Until then I had been trying to show the beauty of people in love. Shocked that love could go so wrong, I became obsessed with documenting domestic violence. Driven to try to do something about it, I found that a camera was my best weapon.

Much of this book was born out of frustration—first, because I felt powerless in the face of the violence I had seen, and second, because for a long time no magazine would publish the pictures. It was only when I received the Eugene Smith Award in 1986 that magazine editors began to take the project seriously.

I felt that it was important to find ways to show as many aspects of the problem as I could because this problem has been concealed from public view for too long.

During the last ten years, I went to demonstrations and conferences, hung around courtrooms and hospital emergency rooms, rode with police, sat in on batterers' therapy groups and women's self-defense classes, and lived in women's shelters and women's prisons. I stayed in the violent homes of the very rich and the very poor—domestic violence knows no economic boundaries.

The text has been taken from my own interviews with battered women, violent men, and activists, and from interviews conducted by reporters with whom I worked on domestic-violence stories. The most daunting task was to find women and men who would agree to expose their lives. I was fortunate to find people who felt that it was vitally important for others to see the nature of the problem.

A few of the people I photographed asked not to be identified by their real names. In all cases they gave permission to tell their real stories and to use their pictures. The lives of many of the subjects in this book have changed. Some have solved their problems; others are still trying. But every one has contributed to my search for an end to violence.

If this book finds a way into your heart, I hope you will contemplate this: There are countless women in prison whose sole crime was to protect themselves and their children from murderous husbands or boyfriends. Many things are shocking about family violence, but none more so than the fact that women are behind bars for trying to save their own lives.

Donna Ferrato
New York City
July 1991

LIVING
WITH THE ENEMY

DONNA FERRATO

INTRODUCTION BY

ANN JONES

APERTURE

LIVING WITH THE ENEMY IS DEDICATED TO THE TRIUMPH OF LOVE OVER
VIOLENCE, TO FREEDOM OVER OPPRESSION, AND TO THE INDOMITABLE
SPIRIT OF WOMEN. DEAR DAUGHTER—THIS BOOK IS FOR YOU. —D.F.

EDITOR'S NOTE *Living with the Enemy* has involved the collaboration of many people, but without the faces and voices of the women who have been ruthlessly terrorized, there would be no book. Each woman agreed to speak with and be photographed by Donna Ferrato, knowing that her story would one day be made public. The extraordinary strength and courage of these women have inspired our profound admiration and respect. In presenting *Living with the Enemy*, we stand with the women and men in these pages who work to end violence.

Aperture gratefully acknowledges the generous support of the Lynne and Harold Honickman Foundation; the Hunt Alternatives Fund (New York City and Denver, Colorado); the Ms. Foundation for Education and Communication, Inc.; the Sophia Fund; and the Time Inc. Magazine Company.

Library of Congress Catalog Card Number: 91-71317
Hardcover ISBN: 0-89381-489-X
Paperback ISBN: 0-89381-480-6

Cover design: Robert Aulicino.
Composition by Pub-Set, Inc., Union, New Jersey.

Printed and bound by Everbest Printing Company, Ltd., Hong Kong.

Donna Ferrato is represented by the Black Star Photo Agency, New York.

The staff at Aperture for *Living with the Enemy* is Michael E. Hoffman, Executive Director; Melissa Harris, Editor; Jane D. Marsching and Michael Sand, Assistant Editors; Andrea Kells, Editorial Work-Scholar; Stevan Baron, Production Director; Linda Tarack, Production Associate; Wendy Byrne, Design Consultant.

Aperture publishes a periodical, books, and portfolios of fine photography to communicate with serious photographers and creative people everywhere. A complete catalog is available upon request. Address: 20 East 23rd Street, New York, New York 10010.

10 9 8 7 6 5 4 3 2

The presentation of *Living with the Enemy* was conceived by, and the photo spreads designed by, Philip Jones Griffiths.

INTRODUCTION

On December 21, 1990, Ohio's outgoing governor, Richard F. Celeste, granted clemency to twenty-five women in the state prison. He announced plans to free twenty-one of them in the first mass release of women prisoners ever in this country. Four others were scheduled to be freed after serving a minimum of two years. As the *New York Times* reported on page 1, all of them "had been convicted of killing or assaulting husbands or companions who the women said had physically abused them."

After reviewing the cases of more than one hundred women, Governor Celeste found that these twenty-five had been "victims of violence, repeated violence." They had been "entrapped emotionally and physically," he said. Yet because Ohio courts, prior to 1990, refused to admit expert testimony about the experience and state of mind of abused women, all of these women who had defended themselves against assaultive husbands, boyfriends, or fathers were prevented from defending themselves in court. Abused and silenced by the men in their lives, they were abused and silenced again by the law. The state locked them away.

That has been standard procedure in our criminal "justice" system, so it took a brave man to do what Governor Celeste did, to do what every governor in the country has the power to do, but no governor has ever thought to do before: to right this commonplace judicial wrong, to free some of these women—these prisoners of sexual politics, these twice-victimized casualties of the ancient war we jokingly call "the battle between the sexes."

Donna Ferrato, who also happens to come from Ohio, has been photographing that "battle" for many years. She can be described as a combat photographer. Her territory is this singular war in which both sides occupy the same ground, this civil war in which women strive for democracy and freedom while men fight to preserve the old regime. In this devastating war the battlefield and the home front are one and the same. And there are no winners. The atrocities and the casualties are horrible. Thousands of combatants are wounded, crippled, disfigured, traumatized, or maimed for life. Thousands die. And like any military combat, this war tears at the fabric of society at large. We all pay for it. We all suffer. We all lose. Is there anyone in America who doesn't know that this moldy old joke—"POW! Right in the kisser!"—is a deadly social problem?

Nevertheless, the first thing you notice about Ferrato's war photos is that you've never seen anything like them. Violence on the battlefields of Vietnam and Afghanistan and violence in the streets of Beijing and Beirut have been documented by some of the world's best photographers. But violence in the home is something else again. Think of war photography and you think of Mathew Brady, Robert Capa, Don McCullin. You think of trenches and tattered uniforms and bloody bandages and epaulets and armored vehicles exploding in flames. Ferrato's images make you think again.

How does she *get* these pictures? That's the first thing people ask, and understandably so. If wife beating has been hidden from public scrutiny since the beginning of time, how does a photographer photograph it? What man, about to beat up his wife or his girlfriend, would do it before the camera? You might as well ask: What man about to shoot a prisoner in the head would do it before the camera? Yet that did happen. Everyone remembers *that* image. If a thing is done, the camera can see it. Everything depends upon where the photographer points the camera. Everything depends—in other words—on who the photographer is and what she sees.

Donna Ferrato is a small woman with the bright face of a curious child. She carries one camera, a funny one—an old beat-up Leica patched with red and green vinyl tape. It is small and quiet, and she doesn't use it often. She'll hang out for days at a hospital or a shelter or a police department or somebody's house—she loves talking to people—and once in a while she'll squeeze off a picture with her funny-looking camera, like any casual observer snapping a souvenir photo on an Instamatic. Wherever she is, she fits right in. When she stayed in a women's prison to photograph inmates, guards wrote her up for questioning a direct order. They forgot she was only a visitor. Ferrato just doesn't match up to anybody's notion of what a professional photographer is supposed to look like or how a professional photographer is supposed to behave. She doesn't carry a bulging Domke bag. She doesn't own combat boots or a safari jacket. She's just a woman. Harmless. We know that many wife beaters assault their wives in front of the children, other family members, friends, neighbors, the police. To such men, one more witness makes little difference.

But then isn't she a kind of spy? Is it *right* that she sneaks into some man's sanctified home and brings out such a record of what goes on there, behind the lines? I've heard a photo editor complain that some of Ferrato's photographs depict things too private to be photographed. Some things should *not* be imaged, the argument goes, and "domestic violence" is one of those things. This argument is put in terms of the ethics or the aesthetics of photojournalism, but the curious thing about it is how closely it approximates the traditional excuse of the law and the church and the state for doing nothing to stop violence against women and children. In 1874 the Supreme Court of North Carolina ruled that when a husband "chastises" his wife, "if no permanent injury has been inflicted . . . it is better to draw the curtain, shut out the public gaze, and leave the parties to forgive and forget." Things not looked at do not go away. They go on and on, undeterred—which is precisely the point. For another century our criminal justice system and public policy continued to draw the curtain and shut out the public gaze, leaving women to forgive and men to forget. How sad, and how ironic, that the camera should be the last to look. For photojournalism the appropriate question is not, "Is this violence too private to be imaged?" The appropriate question is, "Why haven't we seen it before?"

Ferrato covers a real war. Look at the casualty lists. Look at the body count. It is estimated that a woman is beaten in the United States every fifteen seconds. Yet the immense numbers of incidents and victims recorded in the statistical charts are almost certainly too low, because many jurisdictions still don't bother to keep records of "routine" wife beating. Many officers don't write up a report until somebody gets killed. Those reports list 38,648 women and men killed between 1976 and 1987 in what statisticians call "partner homicide." Two out of three of those "partners" killed are women. The third is a man killed by a desperate woman, almost always in her own self-defense. This year, according to minimum estimates, two million women will be *severely* assaulted by their male partners. At least two thousand women will be killed. To escape this violence, thousands of women will kill themselves. Thousands more will "numb out" on alcohol, drugs, and doctor-prescribed tranquilizers. About a thousand more, determined to survive, will turn the tables and kill the men who beat them. Most of those women, convicted of murder, will spend the better part of their lives in prison.

American women suffer more injuries from battering than from traffic accidents, rapes, and muggings combined. Battering injuries account for at least twenty to thirty percent of women's visits to hospital emergency rooms. Battering is an important cause of female absenteeism in the workplace. Battering, not pregnancy or motherhood, is the main reason women leave the work force altogether. Battering of pregnant women is a cause of miscarriage and fetal damage subsequently passed off as "birth defects." Battering is a leading cause of crime among women; thousands are coerced to commit crimes—typically shoplifting, forgery, drug sales, prostitution—to avoid being beaten. The vast majority of women currently in prison were battered and/or sexually abused as children and/or as adults, and most of the women now serving time in prison for homicide killed an assailant to save themselves. Over half of all women murdered in the United States are killed by their current or former boyfriends or husbands.

When women are battered, women are not the only victims. In many cases, batterers abuse the children as well, and psychologists believe that children may be profoundly traumatized by the sight alone of a man abusing their mother. Consequently, woman beating is a contributing cause of alcohol and drug abuse not only among women but also among teenagers of both sexes. Woman beating, a leading cause of suicide among women, undoubtedly contributes to teenage suicide as well. Battering and sexual abuse cause countless youngsters, female and male, to run away from their homes. Battering and sexual abuse of mothers and children are the most common motives when teenaged boys assault or kill their fathers or stepfathers. (Ferrato's photographs and the stories she recounts suggest the appalling violence routinely visited upon children, and the despair of mothers who can neither protect their children nor save themselves.)

Violence that begins in the home doesn't end there. Yelling, threatening, beating, and bludgeoning are "behaviors" that anyone can *learn*. Once a person learns, he can practice anywhere. Children growing up in violent homes get plenty of instruction. They learn the perverse lesson that violence is a quick and effective problem-solving technique—for men—and that women and children are appropriate targets. They learn by repeated example that a violent man nearly always gets his way. The little boy who suffers or who watches violence may become the grown man who practices it, in his own home or in the streets. In fact, battering and childhood sexual abuse lurk in the personal histories of countless men currently serving time in prison for committing violent crimes of *all* kinds.

In short, the economic, social, and emotional toll that battering levies on our society is beyond calculation.

In speaking of this war, social science gives us euphemisms. "Domestic violence." "Spouse abuse." "Partner abuse." "Marital strife." "Relationship discordance." "Familial dysfunction." "Nonverbal miscommunication." Social scientists study these things. You'll notice, however, that these terms conjure no images. Like Orwellian Newspeak, they aim to keep us from seeing what's what. No mention of warfare here. Rather, these terms whisper of insubstantial numbers and vague "social problems," affecting (we must assume) not real individual women but "relationships" and "families," mostly in other people's neighborhoods, in a more or less egalitarian manner. Ferrato's camera, on the other hand, *sees* what domestic violence looks like. Her photographs reveal the simple facts that the jargon is meant to hide.

The first fact to be seen is this: Violence wears a man's face. The assailants, the batterers, the terrorists in these photographs are men. The camera does not single out men for special blame. It merely records the fact obscured by the verbal terminology: At least ninety-five percent of violence committed by "partners" is the handiwork of men.

The bruised and broken faces in these photographs, the tear-streaked faces, terrorized, despairing, defiant faces, are the faces of women and children, both girls and boys. People used to call what goes on in these pictures "wife beating." That term is inadequate too, for it doesn't take in the emotional abuse, the intimidation, the terror that abused women and children know so well. But at least "wife beating" gives a hint of who's doing what to whom. "Domestic violence" is something grown men do to women and kids. In Ferrato's photographs, there's no getting around that fact.

Being clear about who's doing what to whom is important. It also makes people uneasy. It brings us up against some hard truths we commonly prefer to ignore, and it makes us think again about the meaning of simple words like "home" and "family" and "love." By long-standing tradition and legal decision, the door of the American home is closed. What goes on behind it is "private"—a family matter. Within the home, power traditionally belongs to the patriarch, the paterfamilias, the man whose private castle the home is said to be. He can exercise his authority as he sees fit. Americans take pride in that personal, individual freedom—without seeming to notice that it is often the freedom of men alone. It is a point of national honor that no one can tell a "person" what "he" may or may not do within the privacy of "his" home. Even when he maintains his authority by violence, no one—neither friend nor neighbor, police nor court—is supposed to intervene. Certainly no one is supposed to take photographs.

Ferrato's troubling images are bound to raise questions about what "domestic violence" is and why it happens and what can be done to make it stop.

The most important question is: *Why* do men abuse women? And the answer is almost ridiculously simple. Because they can. And because it works.

A violent man gets his way—at least in the short run. The batterer is not simply an angry man. He is not compelled to violence by alcohol or drugs. He does not "lose control of himself," though batterers commonly offer such excuses. He knows what he's doing. His display of anger or violence is a technique he uses to *control* "his" woman—to get her to do what he wants. There are plenty of other coercive techniques one person can use against another: bribery, verbal abuse, lies, withholding of affection or sex or money, threats of abandonment or violence, property destruction, sexual assault, and so on. Women use some of these techniques too, but it's a rare woman who backs up her "nagging" by blackening her husband's eyes or breaking his arm or raping him. And never in history have women been entitled by law to do such things. When a man commits such acts, on the other hand, there's little a woman can do to stop him, except give in. In terms of armaments, the battle between men and women is decidedly one-sided. And for the man who wants everything to go his way, nothing works quite so well as a show of force.

In the long run, of course, violence fails him because it invariably causes the woman—"his" woman—to leave. Spiritually, emotionally, physically: she begins to withdraw. Sometimes it takes her a while to make the break. She has things to worry about—like kids and food and a place to live. And women have been well trained to think every problem is their fault, and their responsibility to fix. Women are adept as listeners, helpers, muses, amateur shrinks, nursemaids, courtesans. Women are schooled in "romance," suckers for a macho man's temporary tears of remorse. Fools for "love." Women try to "work things out." In the process, if the man couples mental manipulation with violence, a woman may be ground down to zero, her mind washed away by the steady drip-drop of psychological abuse. But sooner or later, most women try to say goodbye.

That's where another crucial question comes in: Why don't men let women go? Some do, of course, after the customary legal struggles over property and child custody. But thousands do not. The more a woman tries to get away, the more coercive and controlling the man becomes—and the more dangerous. It's at this point, when she is about to slip free of his precious *control*, that he is most desperate and most lethal. You've seen the headlines: "Man shoots estranged wife and self." You've heard the old cliché: "If I can't have you, nobody can." Men really do *say* that. And many women decide that it's safer to stay where they are, taking an occasional beating, than to leave and get shot. It's a reasonable choice. But at that point they're not really wives or girlfriends anymore. They're prisoners.

Next question: How do these guys get away with it? The answer to that is another question: Who's going to stop them? To assault a woman *because she is a woman* (as in, "You're *my* woman!") is both a crime and a violation of her civil rights. But even at this late date few people, and few of our institutions, see it that way.

We "know" too much about "domestic violence." And most of what we know is false and wrongheaded and damaging to women and kids. All these years, we've blamed the woman. She asks for it. She likes it. She provokes it. She says no, but she doesn't mean it. And even if she means it, she'll come around. If she doesn't like it, why doesn't she leave? We've "known" that "domestic violence" happens only to poor women, or only to women of color, or only to women raised in violent families, or only to women who ask for it. For more than a decade we've handed out tax dollars to social scientists (mostly male) to study statistics. These social scientists devise tests and administer questionnaires to find out: What's wrong with battered women? Why do they make themselves victims? What is their psychological profile?

Finally, after all these years comes the "scientific" answer, the answer that women have suggested all along, with only their common sense and hard experience for evidence. This is the fact: The only characteristic all abused women have in common is that they are *female*. In other words, any woman may be assaulted by a batterer. In other words, women are battered *because they are women*.

But that's not what law enforcement agencies think. "Knowing" that women ask for abuse, law officers have treated "domestic assault" not as an assault like any other assault, but as a private family matter—not a crime, but a "domestic dispute," an argument, a lovers' quarrel, a spat. Until the last few years, official policy everywhere in the United States called for mediation, not arrest—and in many jurisdictions, it still does. Many battered women report that when they call the cops, nobody comes. Some battered women *live* with cops.

The attitude of the police is echoed by prosecutors and judges. In case after case, police declined to arrest, or prosecutors declined to prosecute, or judges declined to sentence batterers who subsequently killed the woman who sought the law's protection. We should not be surprised that every year a thousand women kill a man who assaults them. At the time of the homicide, most of these women have left the assaultive man, or they are trying to get away. Many of them have gone into hiding. Many of them have obtained legal restraining orders or "orders of protection." But the man will not quit. After the homicide, all the women say the same thing: "Nobody else would make him stop."

You'll see such women in Ferrato's photographs—women still haunted by ex-husbands and boyfriends who won't let go. And women who killed to save themselves. Prisons all over the United States, as Governor Celeste found in Ohio, are full of women like that. Ferrato had herself locked up in the maximum-security prison in Missouri to get to know some of them. Most of the husband-killers there have sentences on the order of fifty years or life without parole. They'll never get out of prison alive. Maybe that makes husbands in Missouri feel safe. If you met these husband-killers, though—as I have—you'd probably think, as I do, that they're pretty decent people. One of them was married to a chief of police.

The odd thing is that the criminal justice system traditionally regards the crime of assault as *not* a crime if the assaultive man assaults "his" own woman. But if the woman defends herself, *that* act is a crime, and the criminal justice system will punish her. What we're talking about, then, is not a simple failure or deficiency of law enforcement and criminal justice. What we're talking about is systematic, institutional support of woman beating, and institutional punishment of women who resist or fight back.

Other institutions support woman beating too. Medical science prescribes tranquilizers for battered women in fear for their lives. Psychiatry analyzes the "masochism" that supposedly inspires battered women to "provoke" men to abuse them. Religion preaches a wife's duty to her husband. Films, television, advertising, popular magazines, and romance novels increasingly make sex violent and violence sexy. And all the while the inequities of sexism and racism make it harder for women, especially women of color, to live independently and to provide for their children.

How can men get away with abusing women? How could they not?

As for women's civil rights, haven't they always been a joke? Recall that opponents of the 1964 Civil Rights Act added the category "sex" only to make the bill too ridiculous to pass into law. Recall that the Equal Rights Amendment first proposed in 1922 gets defeated year after year. As I write, Senate Bill 2754, "a bill to combat violence and crimes against women on the streets and in homes," the subject of hearings in 1990 before the Senate Judiciary Committee, dies with the 101st Congress. This bill, if passed, would have encouraged states and localities "to treat spousal violence as a serious violation of criminal law." Among other things, it would have encouraged arrest and criminal prosecution of assaulting "spouses," authorized reeducation programs for judges, and made it a crime for a violent "spouse" to track his wife across state lines. Most important, the bill contained a brief section on civil rights. It noted that "current law provides a civil-rights remedy for gender crimes committed in the workplace, but not for gender crimes committed on the street or in the home." This bill would have provided that remedy. Under the Constitution, all people have the fundamental right to live free from bodily harm. This bill, if passed, would have made it clear that women are people too.

Action against woman beating proceeds from the ground up. Led by women, the campaign is one of the most astonishing social reform movements in the history of this or any other country. It started with women helping women, and it is still growing.

Since 1974 women have established about a thousand shelters and at least as many emergency hotlines to provide refuge, information, and advocacy for battered women. Women have pressured many states to enact more comprehensive domestic-violence laws, some of them remarkably creative—like the law that puts a surcharge on marriage licenses for the benefit of shelters. Groups of battered women have brought class-action suits against police departments and court officials to force them to arrest and prosecute batterers. They have pressured the National Association of Chiefs of Police to change its recommended policy from mediation of "domestic disputes" to arrest of assaultive men. In some states and municipalities women have won by law or public policy a practice of mandatory arrest, detention, and prosecution of batterers. They have established support, consciousness-raising, and political action groups for battered women. They have provided advocates to help women though the intricacies of social service agencies and court procedures. They have set up "reeducation" programs for batterers, sometimes as a compulsory alternative to jail time. They have devised training programs for police, prosecutors, judges, and other public officials. They have introduced domestic-violence awareness programs in public schools to help prevent violence and to help kids already suffering from it. Working with hospitals and child-protective services, they have established advocacy programs for mothers who are unable to protect their abused children because they too are being abused. They have led campaigns to remove incompetent and sex-discriminatory public officials and judges whose refusal to enforce laws against assault has left batterers free, in case after case, to murder. They have developed legal strategies for defending battered women who, while defending themselves or their children, assault or kill their batterers. They have produced a shelf of studies on the history, sociology, psychology, politics, law, and personal experience of "domestic violence"; countless reports on local programs that work and don't work; conferences, films, videos, plays, songs, rituals, and innumerable self-help handbooks. They have organized nationwide to coordinate programs, develop policies, and evaluate accomplishments. They have demanded, coaxed, wheedled, flattered, persuaded, cajoled, threatened, lobbied, badgered, and shamed "the system" to give way. Never before in American history have crime victims, denied redress, organized to establish a de facto system of protection for themselves and other victims. These women, all in all, have effected enormous changes that are only just now beginning to be felt.

Donna Ferrato's camera sees these changes in progress—police arresting assailants, batterers attending groups, women in shelters finding safety, women on their own starting over. But these stark images are disquieting. It's one thing to talk about "domestic violence." It's something else again to *see* it. All at once, the combat photographer's camera reveals the sexual politics of this "social problem." All at once, all those things we "know" about "domestic violence" seem weirdly backward or upside down. Looking at these photographs you have to ask: Why are all these women lying wounded in hospitals, or locked in prison cells, or fleeing in the night, or huddled with their children on cots in shelters? Why are all these women, and their children, forced to run from their own homes? And why are the men who terrorize them free to stay put? Why are they free to sit around and talk with a bunch of other guys about the terrible things they did? How come *they* get to go camping?

You tell me: What's wrong with these pictures?

Ann Jones

THE VIOLENCE

As with all injustices, there is the reality, and there are the myths spread by those trying to deny the reality. I have seen the reality of battered, broken, and mutilated women. Every fifteen seconds in America, a woman is beaten by a man she loves and trusts. Between two and four million women will be severely assaulted by a partner this year. In one out of six relationships in the United States, a man assaults a woman. Such violence occurs at least once in more than half of all marriages.

There is a myth that domestic violence is "mutual" and that countless "battered husbands" are beaten by their wives. But the fact is that men commit at least ninety-five percent of all assaults on partners, according to national crime survey data.

There is another myth—many people believe it—that when a man hits his wife or girlfriend, it's nothing more than a slap. But studies of violent families show that abuse is serious and that it often escalates over time, becoming more intense and more frequent. Domestic violence is the leading cause of injury to women in the United States, accounting for more injuries than the next three leading causes—auto accidents, rapes, and muggings—combined. Fifty percent of women murdered are killed by their present or former male partners.

Myths cannot conceal the truth. Yet when women in shelters and prisons started telling me their stories, I realized that no one except those who have lived through it can fully comprehend the gruesome violence that goes on behind closed doors.

Karen, 20, lives in a shelter in St. Paul, Minnesota. She says:

My nose was swollen but not broken. . . . He took a coffee table and broke that over me. He slammed me against the wall and that's how my head got cut open. My nose bled several times. But mostly he slammed, hitting me in the face. He's six-foot-six, a huge man. He was holding his punches, because I'm sure he could have put me away.

Joni, 30, in her suburban Minneapolis apartment, leans on an artificial right leg. The limb was amputated after her ex-husband shot her. He came to fetch the children for his weekend of custody, and before driving off with the kids, he asked them to call Joni out to his truck. He told her that their kids would be better off dead than with her, and he pulled out a gun. Joni will never forget it.

I saw the barrel of the gun. I was facing him when I saw it. I turned around, and I heard the noise, and then I felt my leg. It was like it exploded, and it got really hot and wet. Then the pain hit. I tried hiding under the trees so he couldn't see me to shoot me again. Then I heard two more shots. He was shooting at my children.

Joni's little boy was hit, but he survived.

Chao, 29, a mother of three, says:

My husband says he wants to have sex. I say no. He drags me across the floor by my leg. He is smiling, but he is angry so his whole body is shaking. He can get so mad. . . . This same thing happened many times. He'd kick in the bedroom door; he'd throw me on the floor and kick me. He'd rip off my underwear and jam his hand inside my vagina. Once he held a knife across my neck. He pointed it at my stomach.

Joanne, 48, is currently serving an eight-year sentence in Minnesota's Shakopee Prison for killing her husband. Her life with him was a nightmare.

He'd be laying in bed drunk and, instead of getting up and going into the bathroom, he'd just lean over the bed and throw up. And it was like, "You get up and clean it up." Well, I was just getting sick, and I couldn't take it anymore. And one day I thought, "I don't care. You can beat me, but I'm not cleaning up that mess. You made it, you clean it up." When he got up to get a beer in the middle of the night, he stepped in it. I never slept—I mean, you're alert all the time, because you never know. The next thing, he had me by the hair and pulled me across that bed and was rubbing and dragging me through it. And he says, "I stepped in that. So I'm going to wipe it up with you." I had it in my nose and in my mouth. So I learned my lesson: You clean it up. You don't leave it.

Later that morning . . . he picked up the baby, and he said with a mad look in his eyes, "You better shut this goddamn kid up, or else I'm going to kill it." I said, "Just put him down." But he kept hanging on to him violently. I thought, "Oh God, he's going to break his little body." And I told him, "Bob, put him down!" I said, "You son of a bitch! That's all you're good for is beating up women and kids."

Minutes later, Joanne grabbed Bob's shotgun, closed her eyes, and with one blast put an end to her husband, her marriage, and a decade of abuse.

Why do men beat women? In her book *Women and*

The campaign to end violence against women works to get the legal system to stop trivializing the crime and ignoring the evidence.

Male Violence, Susan Schechter explains, ". . . men use battering as a way to maintain or establish control. . . . Men also abuse when they simply wish to display power for its own sake. . . . Battering is a way of organizing a relationship so that men continue to feel superior to women." (p. 224) Batterers assert "rights" they think they are entitled to enjoy—rights that men have come to expect, given our culture's long history of male domination.

Traditionally, Christianity authorized a husband's "chastisement" of his wife: Saint Paul's teaching that "the head of every man is Christ, and the head of the woman is the man" (I Corinthians 11:3) is only one biblical text used as justification for this violence. In the fifteenth century, Friar Cherubino's *Rules of Marriage* advised a man how to treat his wife: "Scold her sharply, bully and terrify her. And if this still doesn't work, take up a stick and beat her soundly. Not in rage but out of charity and concern for her soul, so that the beating will resound to your merit." Many women chose to become nuns.

The phrase "rule of thumb" comes from an English law that specified the thickness of a rod a man could use to discipline his wife.

The notion of "man as master" appears in the 1922 first edition of Emily Post's *Etiquette*, in the chapter "The Instincts of a Lady": ". . . her dignity demands that as an unhappy wife she must never show her disapproval of her husband, no matter how publicly he slights or outrages her."

Through religion, social custom, and law, men legitimized their control and power over women, and established the home as a man's private domain. Until recently, American law supported him, refusing to cross the threshold and enter "his castle." For some wives, marriage vows still include a pledge of obedience for better or for worse. And many Americans—including some in law enforcement and the judiciary—still believe that wife assault is a trivial and private family matter, not to be intruded upon.

This attitude is now beginning to change, raising hope for a positive answer to this question: Can we put an end to domestic abuse?

For help or information regarding services where you live in the United States, phone 1-800-333-SAFE, the National Domestic Violence Hotline maintained by the National Coalition Against Domestic Violence.

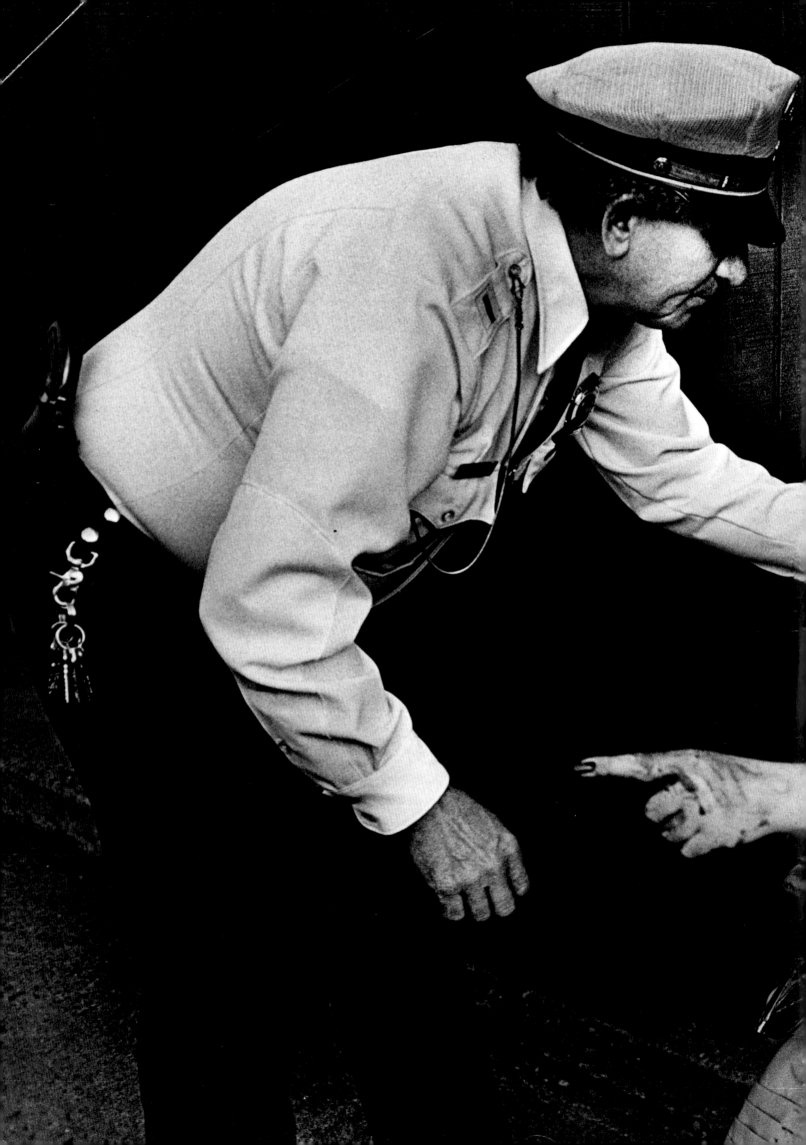

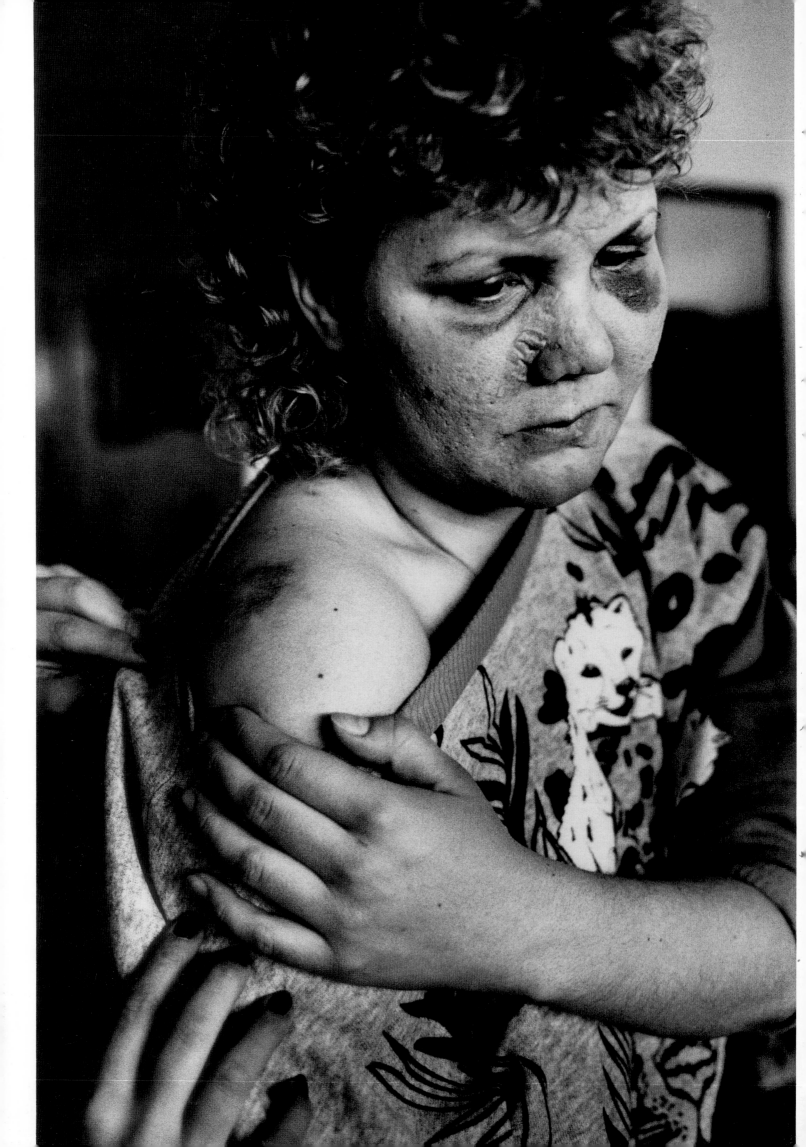

Her friends had suspected something sinister about Richard, but Jane (left), from Minnesota, always defended her boyfriend, who treated her "like a goddess." So Jane was surprised at the attack, although it would be Richard's first and last on her. "He became irrationally jealous. His whole body went into beating me; he used all of it that night. I went to the floor about three times, and each time I got up, he would continue to hit me and kick me over and over. . . . I want everyone to see what he did so the next woman won't be fooled by his Mr. Nice Guy act." Jane had to have facial surgery to repair her nose and cheekbones. She pressed charges. Richard went to jail and then to a court-ordered program for batterers. One year later, he was arrested again for beating a new girlfriend. Pam (above), from California, was assaulted by her husband, who slammed spiked shoes against her head and ground burning cigarettes into her skin, then stabbed her in the hand as their two little daughters stood by helplessly. Robert was arrested but released by a judge who worried that Robert might lose his new job if he stayed in jail too long. Pam and the children went to a shelter. When Robert discovered the location of the shelter, Pam and the children were forced to take refuge at a shelter in another city. (Previous pages:) A McKeesport, Pennsylvania, policeman tried to console a woman who'd been kicked in the head.

When Diana was rushed to a Minneapolis emergency room, her chest was covered with black tire marks. Her boyfriend had driven over her with his truck. In shock and still a little drunk, she tried to remember how she'd landed on the road. She and her boyfriend had been arguing. "He wanted me to get out, but I kept holding onto the door handle. Then I let go. He ran over my chest with the back wheels." And kept going. Diana dragged herself several miles to her grandmother's house. Still in the hospital two days later, she saw her injuries for the first time and said quietly, "Well, I guess I don't look too bad."

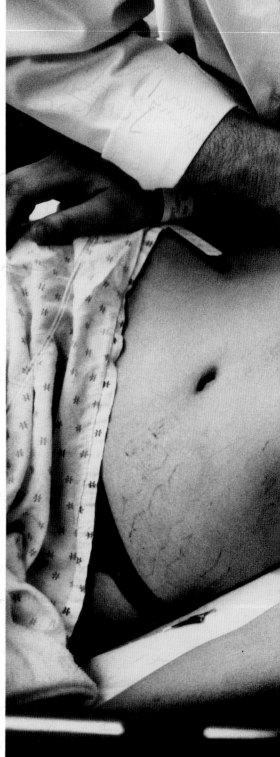

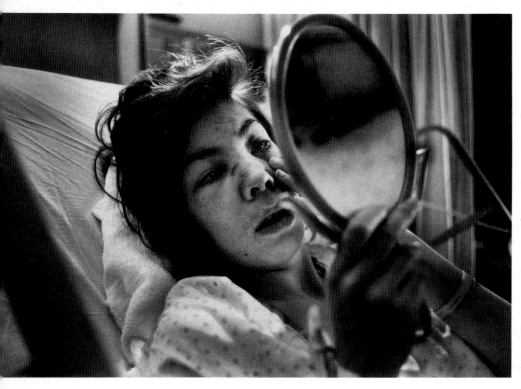

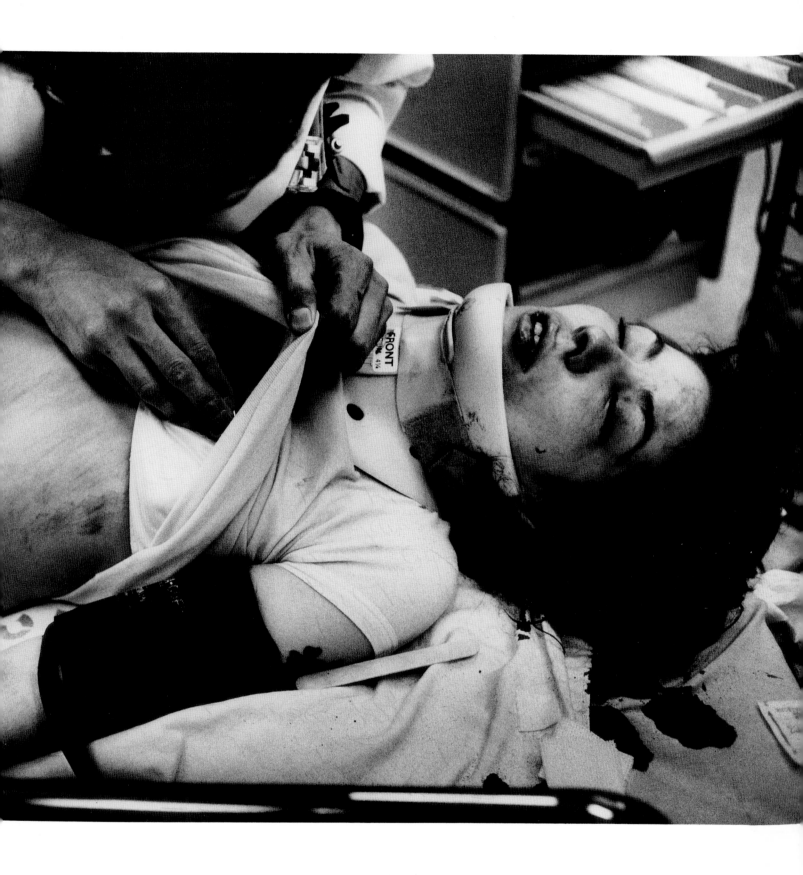

(Overleaf:) Late one night Martha lay in pain with a stab wound in her leg in the emergency room of a Philadelphia hospital. She said, "He didn't mean it. You have to believe that the person you love wouldn't intentionally do this kind of thing."

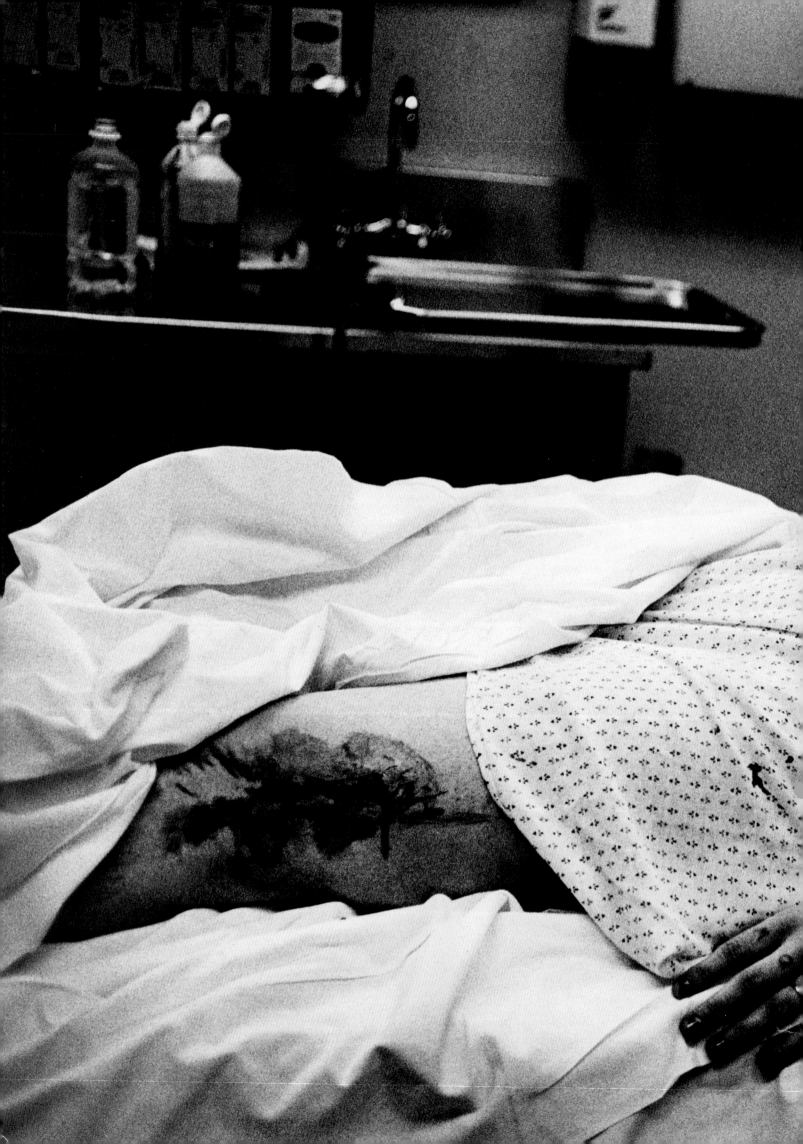

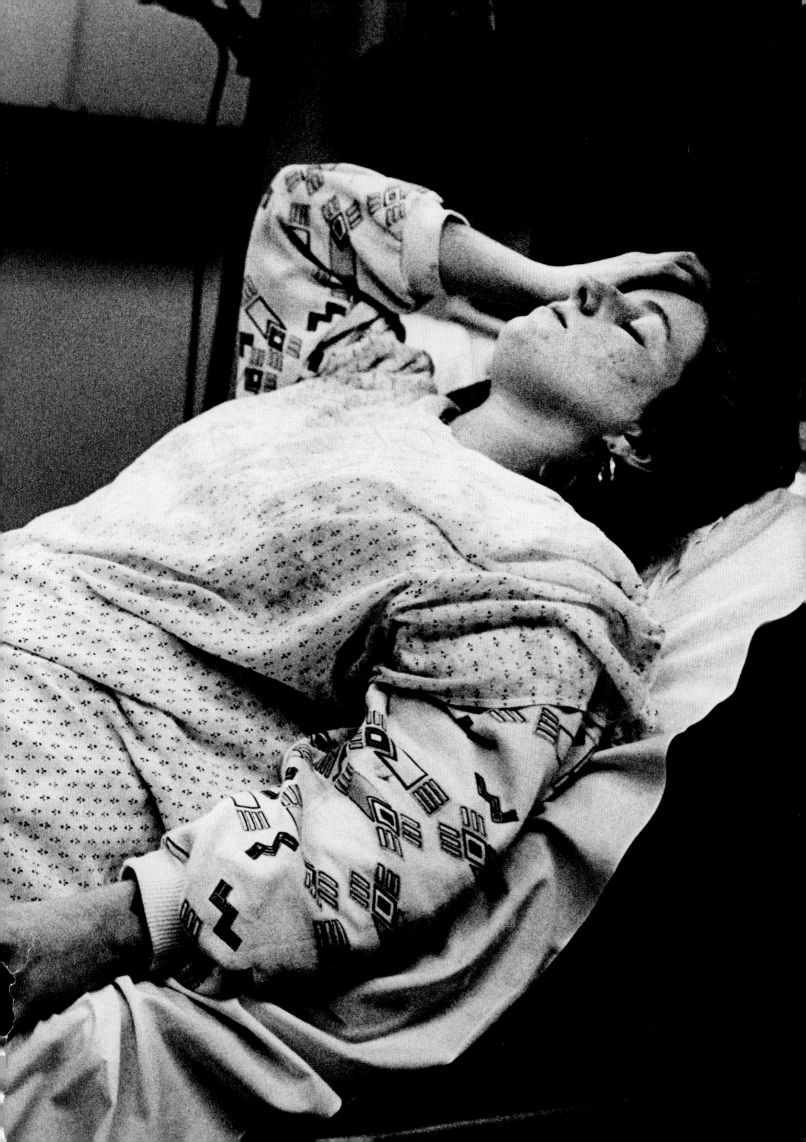

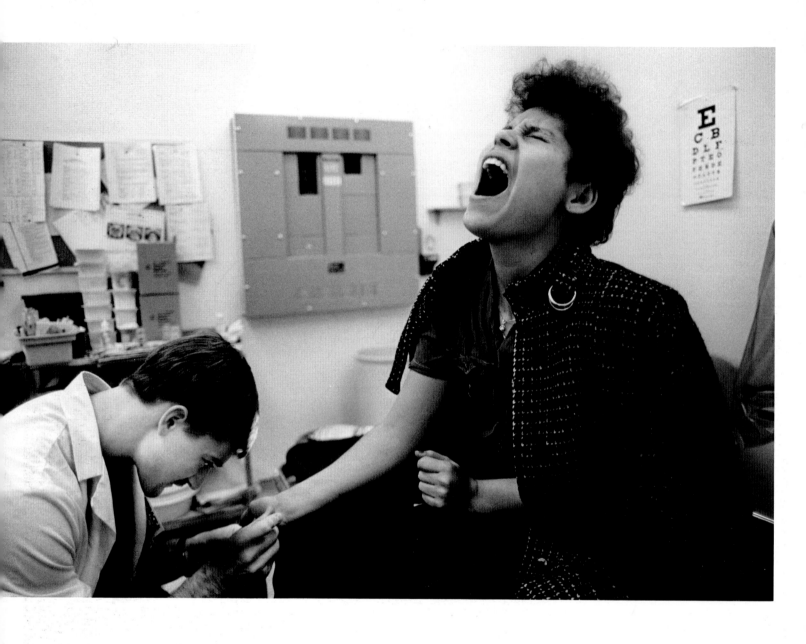

While helping to defend a neighbor from her rampaging husband, Lily (above) was stabbed in the hand. As a result, she permanently lost all feeling in one finger. While she had no regrets about helping her neighbor, Lily, who has three children to provide for, worried that she might miss several days at her job. Absenteeism in the work force caused by domestic abuse is not only common, but costly. Each year it drains the country of three to five billion dollars. Emergency medical services add another one hundred million dollars. When Rita (right) returned home from her night shift in a Philadelphia hospital where she worked as a nurse, her husband, Julio, was waiting for her. It was early morning and her children still had to be dressed for school. Julio accused her of cheating on him instead of working. He punched her in the eyes, smashed her face with the telephone, and broke her nose. The next day Rita's son cried when he saw her. "You don't look like Mommy anymore," he said. Julio was arrested. Rita pushed for protection from her husband, and Julio was ordered to keep away. Now divorced, Rita isn't interested in getting involved with anyone. "It's going to be hard on my own, but I don't want this again."

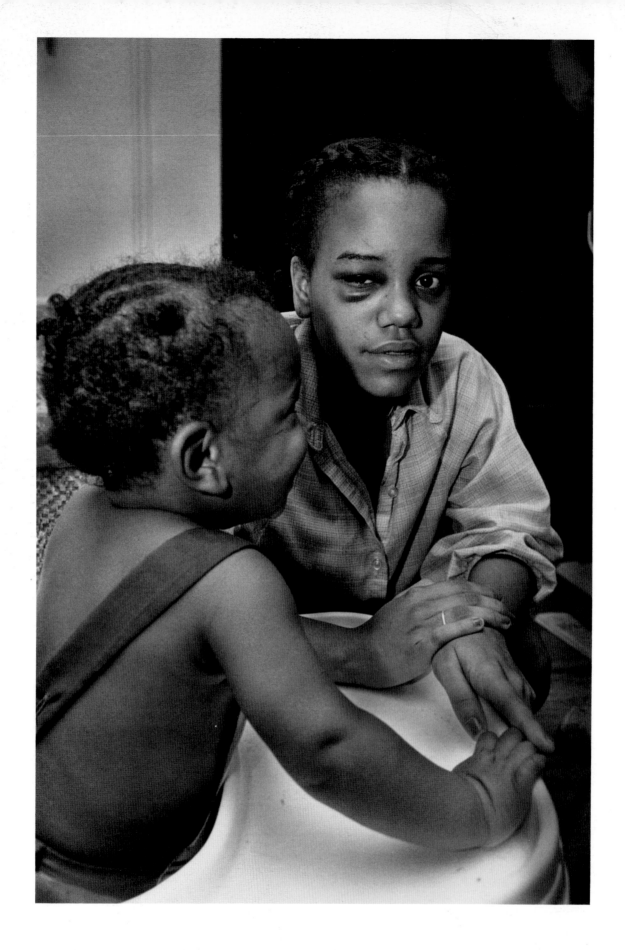

"When he started in on the baby, I had to call the police," Yvonne (above) said. Men who batter women often abuse children, and they in turn may grow up to become abusers. When Tim and Pam (right) married, they believed they were beyond the violence they'd both known as children. Then one afternoon, Tim, who was home alone, couldn't quiet their crying baby. Losing his temper, he shook him so hard that the infant went into a seizure. After the boy recovered, child-welfare authorities decided to put the baby in foster care. The young couple were told their baby could come home when officials were convinced that Tim, court-ordered into a therapy program, could control his violence.

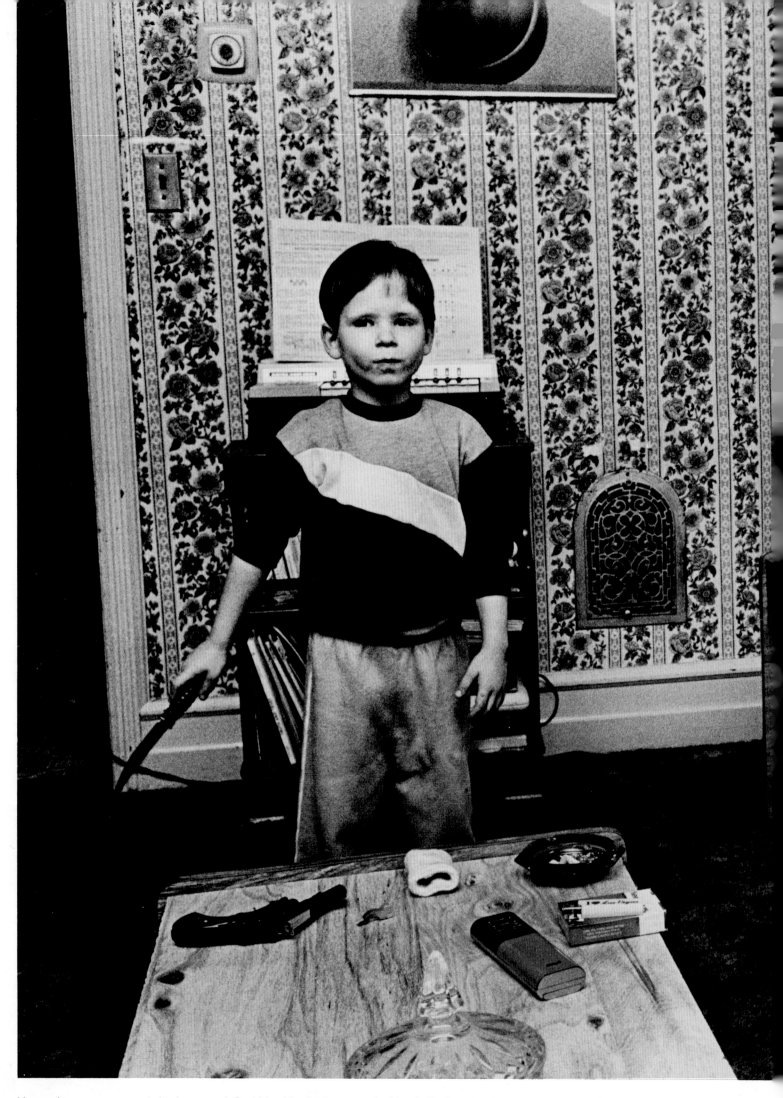

Young Jason never goes to bed unarmed. Grabbing his plastic gun and rubber knife, he tells his mother, "If Daddy comes, I'll be able to stop him."

"I hate you! Never come back to my house," screamed an eight-year-old at his father (overleaf) as police arrested the man for attacking his wife.

THE POLICE

From what I've observed, the police rarely know how to deal with the man who sits calmly in the living room, the picture of innocence, insisting that he didn't do a thing. After all, it's his home. It's his wife. Police don't like entering a man's home and telling him what to do. And many of them also believe that abused women would prefer not to prosecute, and that they will drop the charges.

Many women do press charges, however, in those instances when the police actually arrest the batterer, and a number of women file with the courts for protection and eviction orders. Unfortunately, many others are understandably afraid that if they take action against their partners, the police and courts will not protect them, and the abuser will be encouraged to become more violent.

Often, the police trivialize domestic assault by failing to treat it as the crime it is. Many police officers still say they can't get involved in a squabble between a husband and wife, even when the woman is visibly injured. In general, they don't respond quickly to domestic calls and sometimes do not enforce protection and eviction orders. So the woman's worst fears of repeated violence come true.

Many officers don't see responding to a "10-4," a domestic call, as "real work," or even as part of their jobs. They haven't been trained to regard domestic violence as real violence. At the same time, some police officers often mistakenly believe that 10-4s are the most dangerous calls in their work.

I've seen police get nostalgic for the good old days when there was "real work" to be done catching "bad guys" on the street. That's why they became police officers—not to tell some man to leave his wife alone. Despite widespread changes in police policy, many officers still don't view the batterer as a criminal, although they'd arrest him in a minute if he did to a stranger in the street what he does to his wife at home. It used to be that if a man roughed up his wife a little, the police would advise her to go downtown to police headquarters and lodge her complaint. But realistically, how could a woman leave her home, round up the kids, and find some way to get downtown, with little or no money, no means of transportation, and no concrete proof of her husband's brutality? The criminal justice system required evidence, and if you didn't have it you weren't going to get anywhere with your complaint. The judicial system ultimately discouraged women from seeking ways, within that system, to fight their husbands' abuse.

For years the police have been criticized for not making enough arrests when the evidence was there. And even when they did make an arrest, the judicial system rarely backed it up with any punitive action other than, perhaps, a warning to the abuser not to do it again. Today, however, laws are beginning to change, making it easier to arrest and prosecute these men. The district attorney's office in Philadelphia, for example, reports that the number of such arrests has doubled since April 1986, when the state gave police officers the power to arrest on misdemeanor charges even if they don't actually see the injuries being inflicted. Before this law was passed, a cop had to witness an assault in order to make an arrest. Now, the woman's injuries give the officer probable cause to believe an assault has taken place. Nevertheless, a great deal still depends upon the discretionary power of the individual police officer. Some policemen—and judges—are abusers themselves, so it is not surprising that these men would be of little help to battered women who complain.

One might think that women police officers would do a better job, that they would be more sensitive and responsible in the midst of domestic violence. I'd often ridden with male police officers, but one freezing December night, I had my first opportunity to observe two female officers in action.

The night had been relatively uneventful until a call came over the car computer about a man threatening a woman not far from the police station. We pulled up to the sight of a young blond woman in a thin blue nightgown standing at a pay phone, the thirty-below-zero wind whipping across her body. She was waiting for us. She said her boyfriend was inside the house nearby, threatening her, and she was worried about her baby, who was sick.

We entered the house to find her half-dressed boyfriend, steaming mad. The police said he would have

Activists pressure police to distribute pamphlets about partner abuse and sources of help for women when responding to complaints.

to leave, at which point he grabbed a bottle of pennies and his shirt, but continued to curse and threaten the woman. The officers tried to reason with him, repeating that he would have to go. They watched him dress, followed him outside, and then sat in their heated police car watching as he furiously paced back and forth in front of the house. He shouted that he was cold and had nowhere to go. Finally he stormed down an alley, out of sight of the police. Perhaps he went away, or maybe he just went to the back of the house. The two officers turned their car toward the police station and, when they got there, punched out without writing up a report. I asked why they hadn't made an arrest, or at least filed a report on the incident. "Because it was so close to quitting time for us," one said. "We didn't want to get involved with overtime."

(Previous page:) A battered wife in Philadelphia complained to a police sergeant that her calls for help were rarely answered. Despite a court order to keep away, her husband had broken into her house through the front windows. Another time, as she walked down a street, he sneaked up from behind and began to strangle her. Police have traditionally been reluctant to involve themselves in what many of them regard as private disputes. Activists argue that it's essential to arrest and jail the abuser, not just tell him to stay away. Studies of violent men have revealed that in many cases, jailing, even for one night, deters repeated assaults. According to a Pittsburgh city attorney, "Some men, arrested but not jailed, have gone straight home and beat up their women again while the paperwork was still being processed."

Bruce (right) raged at the night-shift officer, "Why did you arrest me? Her father was attacking me with a broom!" Bruce had been charged with beating his wife. Moments later he broke into tears. Gary (left) was arrested for violating a restraining order issued three hours earlier. He'd been told he couldn't go near his wife while awaiting his trial for assaulting her. But after drinking heavily in a bar, Gary went home "to sleep." His wife called the police. For the next three weeks he slept in jail.

(Overleaf:) The police responded to Mary's call for help and listened to her as she cried that her husband had gone berserk because dinner wasn't ready when he got home from work. They held her husband in another room so she could talk freely. He denied everything, and she said that she was afraid to press charges against him. The police left without making an arrest. As Mary showed the policemen to the door, she whispered, "Remember you were here. The next time, I will be dead."

Some police forces now have specially trained units to handle domestic calls. Officers have learned how to question the parties and detect signs of abuse. In some cities, police officers can arrest violent men if they have probable cause to believe an assault has taken place.

In 1984 *The San Francisco Examiner* reviewed police records from that year's Valentine's Day and found that half the attempted murders in the city on that day occurred within families. Further research showed that the daily average increases forty percent after a Superbowl game.

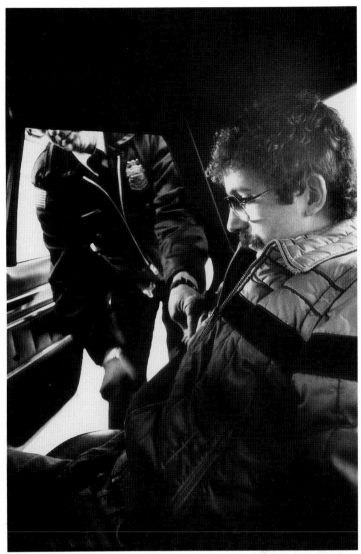

Her husband, Ernie, told police that Myra (left) fell accidentally. "Arrest him, he's a liar," she yelled. As Ernie was led away, he snarled, "Thanks, Myra." "Yeah," she shot back, "thanks for my face, okay?" Ernie had bruised her face and cracked several of her ribs. He was taken to jail, but while there, he had a heart attack. Feeling guilty, Myra decided not to press charges. Another woman said her husband (above) had threatened her, and the Minneapolis police, who treat wife beating as a serious crime, snapped handcuffs onto Travis and took him to jail for the night. She said that Travis never beat her again, but she divorced him anyway.

"He fights all the time, but it was never this bad before," Karen sobbed (overleaf) as her boyfriend was arrested. Her children had been awakened when the boyfriend threw Karen against the bathtub, knocking her unconscious. Later Karen told a battered-women's advocate in the hospital emergency room that she didn't want to press charges. The boyfriend was released from jail the following morning. 45

SHELTERS

Most of what I know about domestic violence I learned from women living in shelters. Most of what those women know about getting free from abusive partners they learned in shelters.

In the 1970s, a group of women set up a phone-in legal service for wives who wanted to divorce. That raised a curtain on a previously unspoken-of world of terror, sadism, shame, and pain. It was clear that many women and children desperately needed safe places to hide out from violent husbands and boyfriends.

In October 1974, in a small apartment in St. Paul, Minnesota, three women—Lisbeth Wolf, Sharon Vaughn, and Cheryl Beardsley—opened the first battered-women's shelter in the United States: Women's Advocates. A movement began that not only has saved the lives of countless women and children but also has changed the way that many of us think about family violence. By 1985 there were 700 shelters. Today there are approximately 1,200 shelters and safe houses in the U.S. Their locations are usually kept secret to protect residents from vengeful husbands.

Shelters provide a supportive environment where women and children can obtain immediate refuge as well as helpful information and services. Many women who enter shelters go on from there to make a new start for their families. Unfortunately, there are still millions of women who live nowhere near a shelter. There are far more animal shelters in this country than shelters for women and children.

Women seeking refuge often arrive at a shelter in the middle of the night, suffering from exhaustion, fear, stress, and physical injury. They are literally running for their lives. It's ironic that these women—the *victims* of crime—are made to live like criminals, hiding in homes with bars on the windows, sleeping among strangers, donning disguises to go out in public, and always having to watch their backs. Their husbands or boyfriends—dangerous, assaultive men—are the ones who remain safe at home.

Marty Friday, director of the Women's Center and Shelter of Greater Pittsburgh, arranged for me to spend time at the shelter and to attend a meeting with the residents. I asked their permission to photograph in the shelter, and they overwhelmed me with their stories. The things they talked about I had thought happened only to prisoners of war—women chained to chairs, their fingernails ripped out, women shot at while sleeping, women raped in front of their children. Many had mixed feelings about being in a shelter; they were happy for the temporary safety, but angry that they had to live like fugitives when they hadn't done anything wrong. At first, it was hard for me to understand their unrelenting fear, since they were now apparently free of their abusers. But the women in Pittsburgh made me realize that once you have an abusive man in your life, it's not easy to be rid of him. "Until death do us part" had taken on new meaning for many of these women.

At that time, the Pittsburgh shelter was located in the basement of a seminary. The walls were peeling and the floor was damp. Sunshine rarely filtered through the barred windows, and when it did the rays revealed a fog of cigarette smoke. Babies cried as mothers took turns with cooking and chores. Nevertheless, this was a wonderfully supportive environment. The women became like sisters, cutting one another's hair, reading books to the children, dancing in the middle of the night with the radio at full volume, taking turns making grand dinners. Most of the time the shelter was filled with lively chatter. But a gnawing sense of fear was always present.

One night I sat with a resident named Kate, who had seven stitches across her nose, a bandaged chest because of three broken ribs, and two black eyes. Although it was very late, she worked at the stove preparing stuffing for the Thanksgiving Day turkey. As she was telling me about the last time she was beaten, her eleven-year-old son came in, rubbing the tears off his face. Under a bare fluorescent circle of light, Kate rocked her frightened boy as he sobbed that he'd had a dream of losing her. They clung to each other with love and fear.

Shelter residents are under enormous pressure: they are thrust into unfamiliar surroundings, and obliged to live among strangers. Educating their children can be a serious problem, since many men try to ambush the mother or kidnap the children as she takes them to or from school. The women usually have little money with them, and they can't go

Driven from their homes by violent men, women and children escape to shelters in secret locations, often in the middle of the night.

to work either, for fear their husbands or boyfriends will track them down. Then there are the daily chores that must be done to maintain the shelter. Exhausted and depressed, the women still wash and wax the floors, clean the bathrooms, cook the meals, and do the dishes. And because shelter stays usually are limited, the women must also spend time looking for new apartments, new jobs, new schools—new lives. All this while trying to avoid being caught, beaten up again, and possibly killed. The question is easy to ask: why don't battered women just leave their abusive partners? Clearly, even with the help of a shelter, leaving a violent man, and leaving home, is not simple.

Yet many women, after staying in a shelter, manage to create a new life for themselves. With fellow residents—new friends—they find apartments to share, and together they set up safety networks in their neighborhoods. They take responsibility for their own and each other's protection, learning how

to *live* in spite of what they're up against.

Some women start to sound and act like guerrilla fighters moving into enemy territory. They vary their paths to work each day and strategize about escape routes. They invent disguises. They get apartments above the ground floor (so the abuser can't come through the window) and, if they can, they settle in the safest counties (measured in terms of police response to emergency calls).

I accompanied one shelter resident on a house-hunting trip. "Mom, there's no bars on these windows," observed the woman's seven-year-old son, as they looked at and rejected a potential new apartment. It seemed odd that a woman who'd struggled to leave one kind of prison would look for a house that actually had bars on the windows. But as the Pittsburgh shelter residents said again and again: once you have a violent man in your life, it's very hard to get rid of him, or of the fear of him.

Pregnant and speaking no English, Lan moved into Women's Advocates in St. Paul with her eight children (above). With the help of another resident, Chao, acting as translator, Lan told an advocate that her husband had been beating and raping her for several years. She didn't know what was going to become of her and the children, but she felt great pride at finally leaving her husband. In a Philadelphia shelter, a young mother (above, right) carried her exhausted daughter to bed and spoke about male-female relationships. "As for what love is, that's what I'm trying to find out now. He'll kick your face in, then bring you flowers and chocolate. You call that love? I call it brainwashing."

There is no typical shelter resident, just as there is no typical battered woman. At Women's Advocates in St. Paul, the country's first shelter, women can stay four to six weeks and have access to legal, financial, medical, and job assistance. The mural in the house was painted by a resident ten years ago (previous).

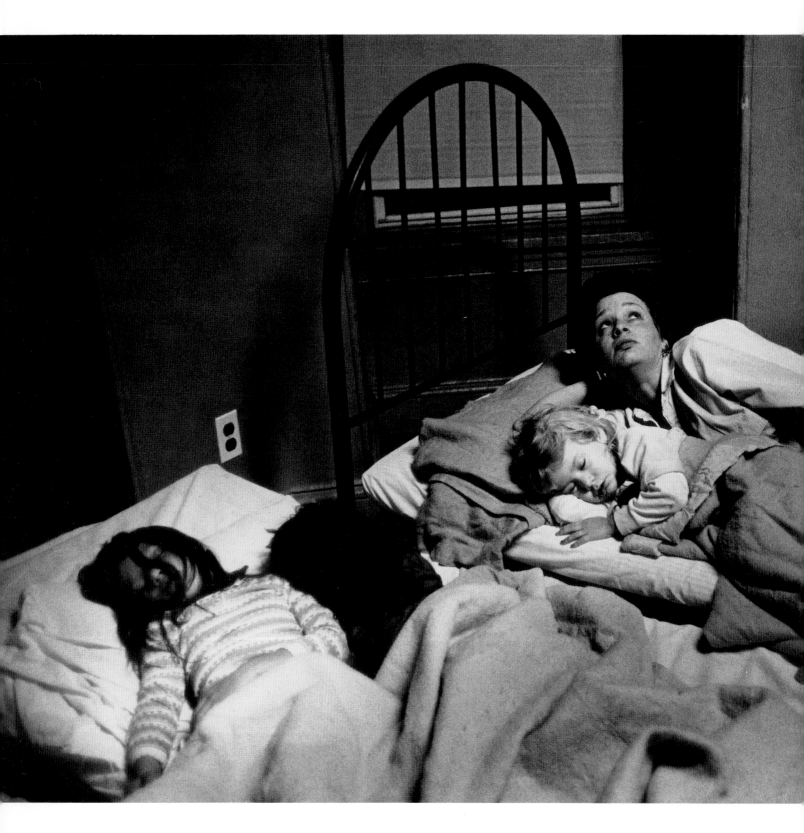

Kim (above, right) feared that the tension she felt at leaving her violent husband and starting over alone was dangerous for her baby. "I could grab him right now, if he did something bad, and throw him up against the wall," she said in her room at Women Against Abuse shelter in Philadelphia. "And at moments like this I think, 'My dad used to do that to me, now I may do it to this kid.' " The staff at shelters help women deal with such feelings. In her room at an inner-city shelter, a young mother (above) kept the lights on through the night and her eyes on the roaches crawling the walls. Many shelters can offer only poor accommodations, because of a lack of funds.

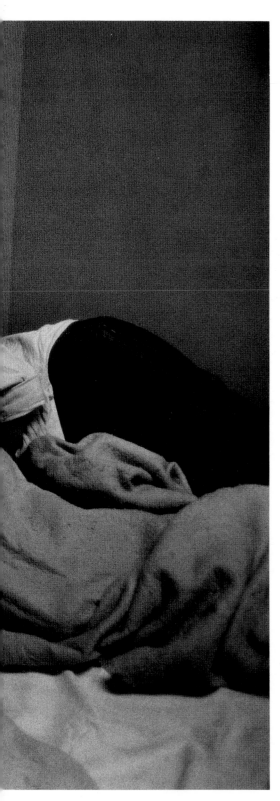

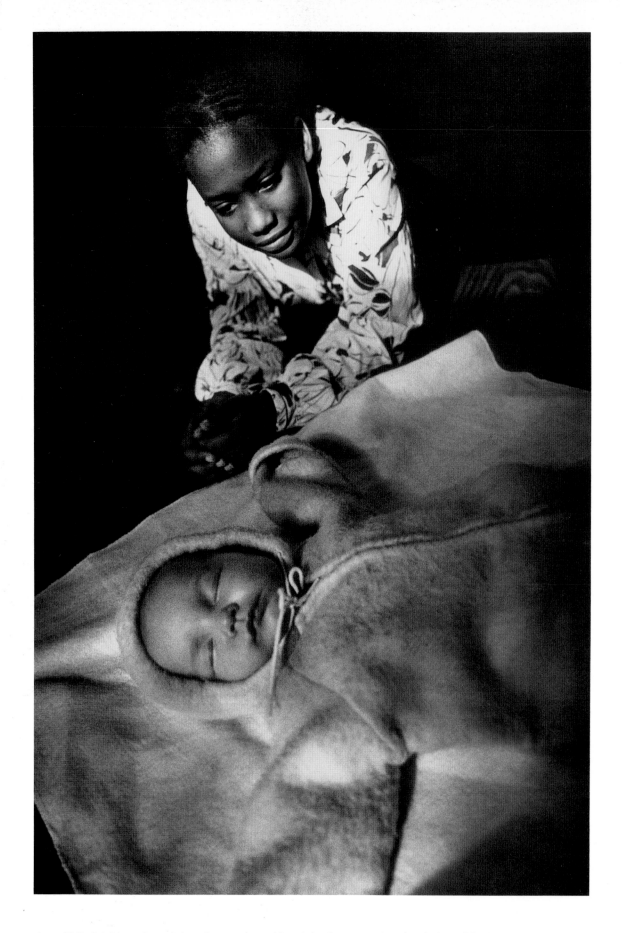

At a Philadelphia refuge (above), a young girl watched over a sleeping baby while his mother worked in the shelter's kitchen. A mother and her infant son (right) slept peacefully after arriving at the Women Against Abuse shelter. The next morning she said, "It was our first safe night in a long, long time."

The first phone call home can be dangerous, especially when a woman's time in the shelter is running out and she has no place to go. The man cries, "Baby, where are you? I've been going crazy without you. You've got to come home, baby. Baby, I love you." Hearing things she wants to believe, a woman may be overwhelmed with confusion. Her resolve to stay away may weaken.

Seven-year-old Shanna tried to comfort her mother (left), who was talking about the two years of abuse she suffered at the hands of a boyfriend. The next day they moved into a two-bedroom apartment near a good school. Unfortunately for many women, abusive men often try to prevent them from starting a new life. Kate (above) was in hiding from her boyfriend, who'd hurt her several times. He tracked her down by tricking one of her children into giving him the address. The boyfriend broke through the front door and went after Kate, shoving her against cupboards, breaking her nose, kicking and punching her, breaking her ribs, and blackening her eyes. While the boyfriend splattered Kate's blood across the kitchen, her deaf and mute daughter watched in silent terror.

Suspicion and fear are common among children who have lived in violent homes. Many who seek refuge along with their battered mothers are seriously troubled. Anna (top) had seen her father burn and stab her mother. While she waited to go to another shelter with her mother and sister, Anna kept her eye on the street, frightened her father would find them before they could get away.

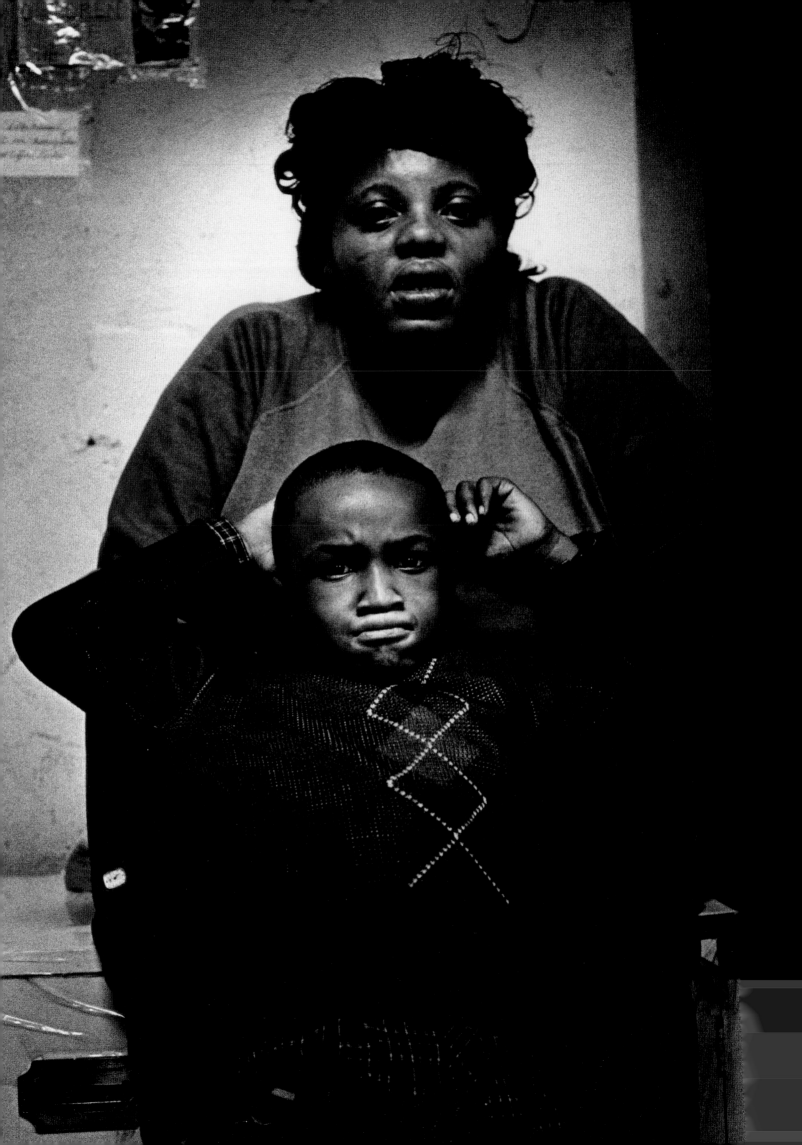

After Mary's husband, Lawson, held a shotgun to her head and threatened to blow it off, Mary took her three daughters and ran to a shelter. The next day she filed a complaint against him, secured a restraining order, and sued him for divorce and custody of their children. Charged with assault, Lawson was given two days in jail, a $165 fine, and a year's probation. Said Mary, "I tried to press attempted murder charges because he tried to kill me that night. But the lawyer said he couldn't do it, that it was only domestic assault, since I'm his wife." Lawson was seen driving around in the neighborhood of the shelter. Mary was terrified her husband would try to punish her. With help from some of the other women in the shelter, she dyed her brown hair blond (below) in the hopes Lawson wouldn't recognize her. Her daughters adjusted quickly to life in the shelter. As Mary slept, they played with her makeup (left). They showed no emotion as they studied a photo of the family together.

Many shelter workers have observed that daughters who see their mothers beaten become quiet, depressed, and withdrawn. Mary understood this and she became determined to break the chain for the sake of her three daughters. First she undertook what for her was the most difficult task—she sent her daughters off to live with their grandmother in order to protect them (above). Then she set about evaluating her situation and before long started to see herself as a victim not only of her husband but of the legal system that would not punish him or protect her. Finally she got away from her abusive husband, returned to school, and now works with children of addicts.

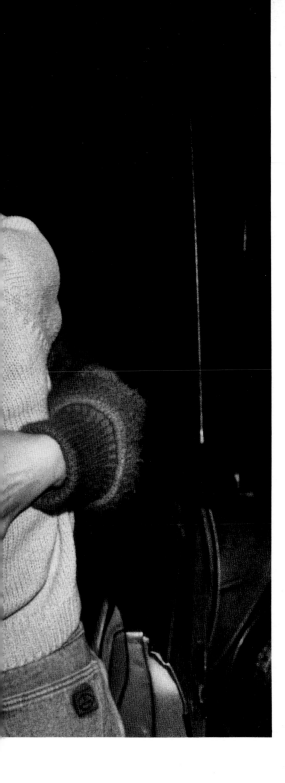

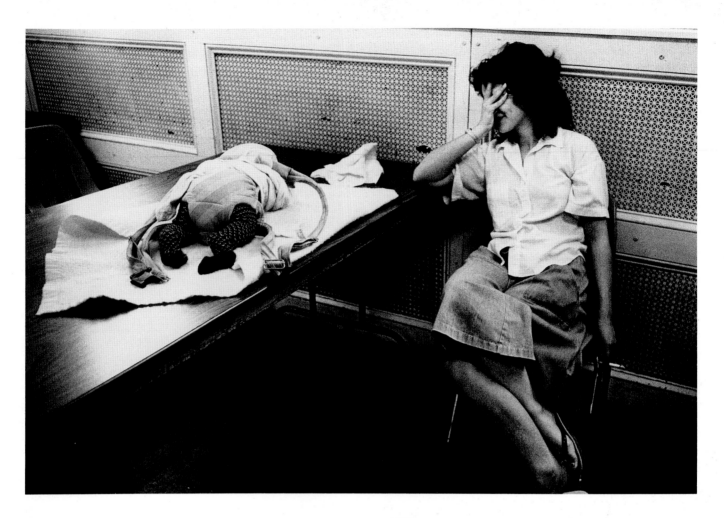

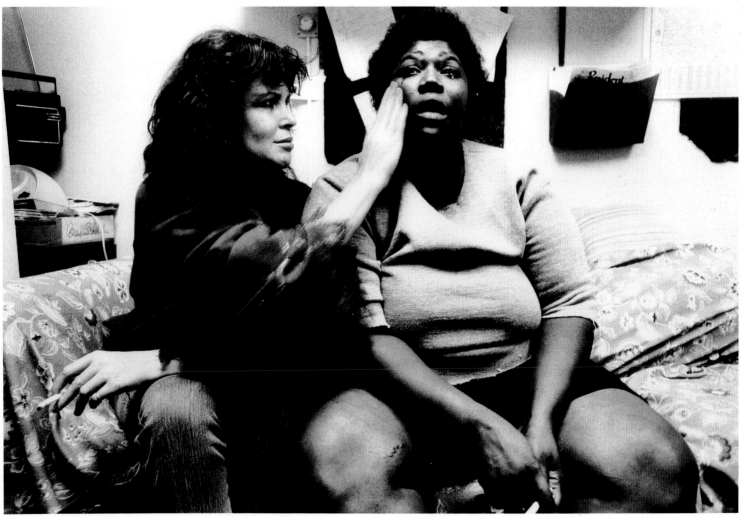

Often, after experiencing traumatic events, a battered woman feels too humiliated or terrified to tell anyone what's happened to her. She thinks no one will help her. In the shelter, women discover there are many other women in a similar situation. Together they discuss their experiences and they help one another. A new solidarity develops and some of the friendships last a lifetime.

Around midnight, when the children are finally asleep, women take time off for themselves. Over cigarettes and coffee, with the music turned up

loud, they let loose, laugh, and talk about what they've been through and what the future will bring. Sharing information helps them overcome.

WOMEN FIGHTING BACK

Some feminists use the word "empowerment" to explain the process of oppressed women taking charge of their lives. I saw scribbled on a shelter wall in Denver a reminder to residents: "Empowerment is a process that aims to reduce the powerlessness of the individual. The goals of empowerment are to learn how to take care of oneself . . . and to become involved in the creation of a better environment . . ."

How can women create "better environments" for themselves when the men who promise to love them turn home into a battlefield?

The flight to a shelter may be a battered woman's first step toward empowerment. There, a woman who has left her violent home, if only for a momentary breath of peace and safety, can get valuable information that may help her to make changes in her life. She may decide to return home again, and then go back to the shelter, making two or three round-trips until she is ready to start out on her own. The information and encouragement she receives in her support group plays a big part in that process.

Women can fight back by acting independently and taking responsibility for their lives. And women do fight back collectively, working for themselves and other women. The battered-women's movement works on restructuring the legal and social systems to aid in the creation of "better environments," where women and children can find safety and respect.

Nationwide conferences, such as the "Battered Women and Justice" conference convened in St. Louis in 1988 by the local Women's Self Help Center, reflect a determination to increase public awareness of domestic violence, to promote prevention through education and training, and to uphold women's rights to safety and justice.

Women go on to fight for the rights of their children. Pat Paterson went to Project Safeguard in Denver for protection and for help in working to change local legislation regarding the rights of custodial parents. Pat's husband had been violent with her, and he had also been convicted of raping her mother. Due for parole, he demanded visitation rights with the children. At the time, Colorado courts were obliged to allow visitation to the father—in this case, a rapist and batterer—unless the mother could prove that he was a danger to the child. So Pat went into action. Her work led to the passage of a bill that shifts to the felon the burden of proving that he is not a danger to the child. Pat's initiative is only one example of a woman taking charge of her situation and not backing down before an intimidating judicial system.

Each woman in this book came to the realization that as long as she was living with the enemy, she was living in danger, and under a constant threat that "it" will happen to her, again and again. These women left their abusive partners and are fighting back.

Activist Esta Soler argued, "This country has depoliticized violence against women. We have to put politics back into the movement."

In this support group in Philadelphia, more than fifty formerly battered women meet weekly with advocates to talk and learn from each other

that they're held down not only by men's violence, but by many institutions of male-dominated culture, such as the law, medicine, and education.

Women attending the "Battered Women and Justice" conference in St. Louis confronted a police official attending a police convention in the same hotel (above). They argued before a group of police officers that the state's standard law-enforcement policies were dangerous to battered women. During a 1986 divorce hearing, Jerry Utesch, an Aurora, Colorado, police officer, pulled his service revolver and shot his estranged wife's attorney, Jeanne Elliott (above right), four times. He had threatened his wife and Elliott before the hearing and although they reported the threats to the police, nothing was done to protect them. Elliott was left paralyzed from the chest down and no longer practices law. She is now a board member of the Domestic Violence Institute in Denver and a courtroom referee in domestic-violence cases who continues to work for women's rights.

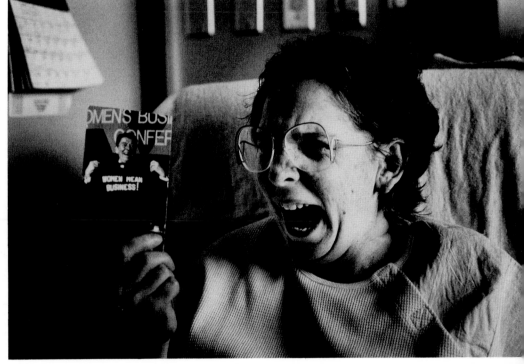

Joni (above) briefs her attorney during her husband's trial. He was sentenced to five to eight years for attempted murder. He'd shot her leg off while "aiming for my vagina." He swore that when released, he would "finish the job." Rallying for women's rights in California, advocate Pat Kuta (top)

lectured police about violence against women, and in Monterey, advocates (top) protested the parole of a man convicted of multiple rapes and murders. Activists Ann Symmington and Nikki Craft (above) led a demonstration against the Miss California beauty pageant in San Diego.

Calling it the "Myth" California contest, demonstrators (above), including radical grandmothers (above left), converged outside the annual state beauty pageant to call attention to what they see as sexual exploitation of women. They use innovative ways of putting their message across, including lots of humor. The serious message is that seemingly innocent beauty contests encourage men to see women as objects that can be owned and abused.

Enlisting the help of their local police force, Joan Sargent and Michael Paymar of the Duluth Domestic Abuse Intervention Project filmed reenactments of typical domestic disputes showing how officers should properly respond (above). The training film is used by law-enforcement agencies across the country. A Boston self-defense course (above right) used men portraying rapists to attack the women participants. The women were taught strategies to fight back effectively (overleaf). Shouting, "No, no, no!" Caroline kicked a well-padded attacker.

BATTERERS

During the last twenty years, many community mental health agencies have developed treatment programs for batterers, sometimes with the help of feminists from the battered-women's movement. Some men have also formed groups of their own—such as EMERGE in Boston, RAVEN (Rape and Violence End Now) in St. Louis, and AMEND (Abusive Men Exploring New Directions) in Denver—to work to end abuse in male-female relationships.

At AMEND, partner abuse is defined as:

Physical: slapping, shaking, shoving, kicking, hitting, biting, scratching, or the use of a weapon or something used as a weapon

Verbal: excessive yelling, frequent criticism, name-calling, threats to assault, or threats to abandon the relationship

Emotional: berating and discounting one's partner in speech or action, refusing to share feelings, neglecting to hear the other's feelings, or giving insulting negative feedback

Sexual: forcing an intimate to have sex or intentionally hurting the partner before or during intercourse

I visited AMEND and spoke with Michael Lindsey, who heads the program. He reports, as many other programs have found, that men may stop physical abuse if they face arrest and sentencing, simply because they don't want to go to jail; but they continue to abuse women and children verbally and emotionally. About fourteen percent of abusive men, Lindsey says, have actually considered killing their wives. About eighteen percent admit to having committed life-threatening violence (for which the sentence may be as light as ten weeks of psychotherapy). These men are dangerous and should be monitored, Lindsey insists, not for weeks but for years. He says, "They need to be told, 'You've got to watch it. You screw up and you're going to go to jail.'"

Nevertheless, Lindsey says, "Judges are loath to give these men heavy consequences. It's as if judges say, 'These poor men! If they have to go to jail, they might lose their jobs.' But the kind of men we're talking about are criminals. If they attacked someone on the street, judges wouldn't be saying, 'These poor men.' They wouldn't be sending the attacker and his victim together for couples counseling. But I can sexually assault my wife or my ten-year-old daughter and I'll be sentenced to only a few months of family therapy. Abusive men are con men, and they are very good at conning everyone—especially judges. But if you really talk about recovery for these men, you're looking at one to five years in treatment."

I asked Lindsey if it would be possible for me to live with and photograph families who had a past record of domestic violence and who were trying to work through their problems with the help of his group at AMEND. He discussed it with some of the batterers, who then discussed it with their partners. Three couples agreed: Neil and Wendy, who have a large Mormon family; Jim and Karen; and Bob and Faith.

The following week I went to Denver, to attend my first session with an AMEND group. I sat on the floor with six wife beaters and Lindsey. The room was very dark and had an air of intimacy. My camera was an intrusion. There was an awkward silence. Then, when the men began to feel the camaraderie of the company of other violent men, they told gruesome stories.

I attended the weekly AMEND group, and went on an Outward Bound weekend trip with couples and group leaders from AMEND and from the local battered-women's shelters. And I moved in with Bob and Faith to begin to document a once-violent relationship on the mend.

Bob was a carpenter and Faith a homemaker who was pregnant. They seemed very tender with each other, very much in love. It made perfect sense that they would want to do everything possible to save their marriage. But occasionally, when Faith was apart from Bob, she said that she was still fearful. Like many other wives of AMEND batterers, she didn't know how to adapt to her "new" husband who was learning to "control" his anger. The men in the group somehow seemed to be hiding their real feel-

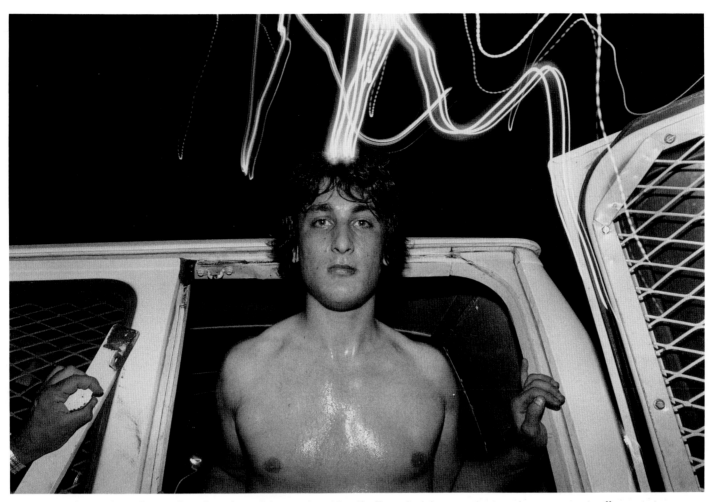

Bruce was taken to the police station after a late-night attack on his wife. To curb violence, experts agree, men must suffer consequences.

ings. Like the other wives, Faith worried that her husband's violence was still there, but hidden.

When Faith and Bob brought their newborn son home, Bob played the proud papa and quickly learned how to change diapers. It seemed as though the bad times were behind them.

A year later, however, I got a letter from Faith saying that the marriage was over. She wrote that Bob hadn't been able to stop trying to control her: he had taken up his old violent behavior again. "The baby and I have moved to our own little house," she wrote. "I'm learning how to be a single parent—we are actually quite a content family. When Bob comes into the picture, the story changes. He has been a never-ending source of trouble. I had to get a restraining order against him because he would not leave me alone. I had a friend over one night, and Bob was outside watching us through the window." Michael Lindsey acknowledges that the success rate at AMEND is only one percent.

Facilitator Frank Snelling (above) moderates a court-ordered counseling session for batterers in Monterey, California. Todd (in AT&T
cap) was called out of a weekly court-ordered group session for wife
beaters in Minnesota by his parole officer and returned shaken. To
the group of men (photos left), ranging in age from late teens to fifties,
he announced, "She just got a restraining order against me. I went to
her house on New Year's Eve afternoon and found her in bed with
another man. I was more than upset. I'm still in shock. But I walked
away. Two years ago, before these classes, I would have killed both
of them. I mean, I would be in Stillwater Prison now." The group
facilitator, John, asked, "We don't need to worry about you going after
her now?" A chorus of male voices clamored, "Stay away. Stay away!"

Counseling programs for abusive men, like the one Bill (above right) attended, teach men to take responsibility for their behavior, and to change it. Most participants are ordered by the court to join the group. Often programs last only a few weeks. Bill cried as he admitted to the group that beating his wife reminded him of his father, a violent man who sometimes turned his attacks on Bill. He grew up in fear of his father's unpredictable rages. Once his father threw him across the living room into a wall, leaving Bill deaf in one ear. Now, in front of his therapy group, Bill wept because he recognized there was little difference between the man he had become and the man he had dreaded as a young boy.

Neil broke into tears during his AMEND group meeting. After he had been in counseling a few months, he and Wendy were reunited. Many men

use counseling as a ploy to persuade their wives to return, and women do return more readily to men in counseling, expecting changed behavior.

Neil and Wendy (above) were devout Mormons living in Denver. It was Neil's second marriage and it had lasted eight years when one night he assaulted Wendy. He accused her of criticizing his teenage daughters from his previous marriage. In the kitchen in front of their children, Neil began to choke Wendy. Wendy left with their three sons and moved to her sister's house in another state. Neil was shaken by her departure and turned to his local Mormon Church for help. The elders offered no advice. He was desperate by the time he enrolled in the AMEND program.

Neil and Wendy (top) at home in Denver during one of their reconciliations. On this occasion they took Neil's attempts at solving his problem seriously enough to visit a local bookshop together. They tried to find books that would shed light on the causes of his violent behavior.

They both shopped for Christmas decorations (top) and later, with his family around him, Neil conducted family prayers (above and overleaf). He begged forgiveness for the abuse he had committed. Shortly after, he dropped out of the AMEND group and left no forwarding address.

Karen was unhappy ironing clothes on her day off, especially since Jim had been free the day before and had promised to help her with the

housework so they could enjoy time together. Disputes about house duties head the list of marital quarrels. Money, sex, and children follow.

At 2 a.m. a light clicked on in Jim and Karen's bedroom. They argued about Jim's upcoming business trip. Karen cried about his past infidelities. She did not want him to be unfaithful again. Jim tried to reassure her he had changed, that he loved her and had no intention of being unfaithful. Karen rejected his assurances. Finally Jim tried to embrace her, but Karen folded herself into a stiff fetal position, and she warned him, "You have been taught that you can't force me in any way—not even to be affectionate." Jim let go. The light went out.

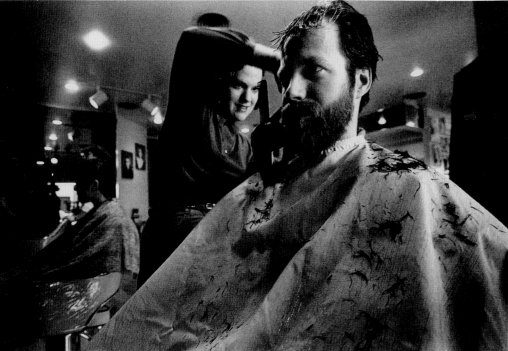

"There aren't very many women I respect; I look at them as pieces of meat," said Bob (top left). As a child he had watched his father beat his mother, but the experience left him angry at his mother, not his father. "My mother did try to leave him three times. In those days a woman wasn't supposed to do that. Her own mother told her to go back to him. She went and talked to the priest. He told her to go back and make the best of it. I know it was hard for her to leave him, but I'm angry with her anyway for not telling him, 'I'm going to leave you if the abuse doesn't stop.'" Not long after Bob and Faith (above left) married, Bob hit Faith, just as he'd seen his father do. Unlike his father, Bob is learning to take responsibility for his behavior. "It's going on three

and a half years now since I've been in therapy for being violent with my wife," he said. "It will probably take me another five or ten years of therapy to get where I want to be. I made changes really fast in the beginning — I was able to stop being physically abusive with Faith after the first few months in therapy. But it's all this other stuff that is taking so long, like my need to control . . . everything. I try to control the family finances, for example, instead of sharing the managing. Then Faith feels like she is losing control." Faith said that Bob's efforts to control her life grew intolerable after the arrival of their firstborn (above). Faith left not long after. She had to get a restraining order against Bob, who had once again become hostile, threatening, and violent.

During an AMEND Outward Bound trip, women led their blindfolded partners along trails in the Colorado Rocky Mountains. "Everyone thinks these men are strong and powerful, but they're some of the weakest, most fragile human beings," explained AMEND's director. "They have tremendous facades. They don't trust. They try to control everything because they're terrified. So you take them to a place that is totally alien to their way of living. This helps to break the shell. They're forced to trust their lives to those they've abused."

ROSALYN'S STORY

Rosalyn was in the bedroom ironing a shirt for her second son, David, then two years old. She knew that she was supposed to wake her husband Roy the next day, but she couldn't remember the exact time. "What time do you want me to set the alarm clock?" she asked him. Irritated, Roy responded that he'd already told her on the telephone a few days before. "Well, I forgot," she said. "Tell me again."

Roy leapt out of bed, grabbed her by the neck, and pinned her down. He began punching her in the face. Rosalyn says, "I kept praying as he was punching that he wouldn't grab the hot iron and use it. . . . For some reason, he stopped and went out of the room. I called the police. When they arrived, Roy was calm and collected. The police asked him to come out and answer questions. He told them I was behaving hysterically because I was having my period." The police offered to take Rosalyn to the hospital. "Of course, I didn't want to leave my children alone with him, so I declined. As soon as the police left, he went crazy again. The police took much longer to return. My husband promised the police he would leave and go cool off. So they left. After that, he stomped around the house saying nobody was going to make him leave. But eventually, he did."

The next day, Rosalyn went to sing in church, but she couldn't move her mouth because of the pain in her jaw. The pain continued, so she went to see a doctor, who asked her if her husband had hit her. (Two weeks earlier her doctor had been trained by advocates from the Women's Center and Shelter of Greater Pittsburgh to watch for signs of domestic assault and discuss it with his patients.) She told him what had happened. The doctor recommended that she get an X ray and then go to a shelter for battered women. She took the phone number he offered and called the hotline from the hospital. The hotline operator told Rosalyn that she could bring the children to the shelter, but Rosalyn was worn out and in pain; she went home instead. That night, as she lay in bed with the sheets pulled up over her head, listening to Roy shouting and throwing things around the house, Rosalyn thought, "He could kill me tonight." The next day she moved into the shelter.

Rosalyn grew up a devout Catholic. When she met Roy he was a Protestant minister, married with three children. She says, "When I became pregnant with his child, he wanted that to happen, like, to thumb his nose at his colleagues at the church. He divorced and married me. He was determined to be a firm disciplinarian with our first son, Joseph, to teach him the meaning of 'no.' Roy frequently hit him, but I was insulated from how it was damaging him until one day, when Joseph heard his father's van come up the street, he flung his arms across the doorway and cried, 'Mommy, don't let him in!' "

Religion was Roy's most insidious weapon. After Rosalyn had been in the shelter for two weeks, she received a phone call from him. He berated her: "You have forsaken your Christian beliefs. Your duty is here beside me."

All through her life, Rosalyn had tried very hard to win the respect and love that she felt were denied her in her childhood. "I wanted to go to college. But after my father died and my brother and sisters finished college, there was little money. I secretly tried out for beauty competitions to get scholarship money. I wanted to better myself." Rosalyn did win beauty contests, and finally she won a small scholarship to Clarion University in Pennsylvania, from which she graduated in 1971.

When I first met Rosalyn, she was getting another kind of education. In the hallway of the Pittsburgh shelter, she was sitting on the floor with Debbie Krochka, an advocate for battered women. It was her younger son's birthday. Roy had sent no card, nor had he even mentioned the day. Rosalyn had no money to prepare a party, and she was distraught that David would miss out. Debbie promised her, "We'll make the party together. The freezer is full of birthday cakes donated for the children. There are decorations. We'll find some presents." Rosalyn cried as she explained, "I never could go to my mother when I needed help. Nor my husband. This is new to me, feeling that I don't have to do everything myself."

Rosalyn is now remarried, to a legal-aid attorney. She has become an ardent spokeswoman for battered-women's rights in Pennsylvania.

"Changing your life is not like slipping out of wet clothes into dry clothes," she says. "You have to work at it. To get where I've gotten today, I've had to experience real hard times."

Rosalyn's ex-minister husband tried to beat into her ideas of how a good Christian wife should act. She learned to stand up to him.

(Previous pages:) Rosalyn had trouble asking for help. After four weeks in a shelter, she panicked about her son's upcoming birthday. She wanted to give him a party. A counselor found Rosalyn in a hallway, upset that she had no money and that her children were being deprived of everyday childhood experiences because of their father, who hadn't even sent his son a birthday card. The counselor assured her that the center was equipped to handle such occasions, with everything from cake to balloons.

While still living in a shelter, Rosalyn took her sons Joseph and David to a restaurant for dinner. When the hostess inquired, "How many of you will there be?" six-year-old Joseph cried, "There used to be four. Then my Daddy got mean. Now there's only three." Later they visited a fair (left), which Joseph failed to enjoy. Rosalyn explained to him that it was natural to miss his father at such times. Preparing for his second birthday, David got a haircut in the shelter from one of the resident mothers (below).

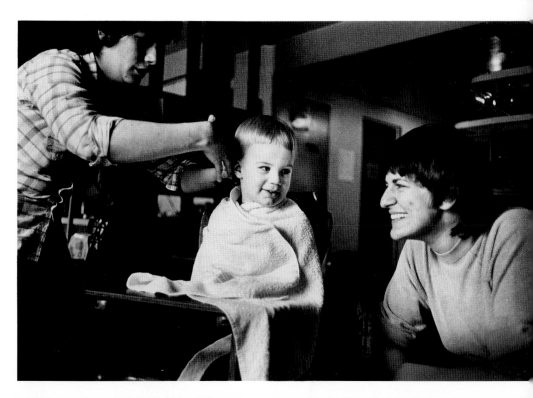

After Rosalyn moved into the shelter, her husband changed the locks on their house. Since she had fled quickly, taking only a few belongings, she went back for her things and had to break through a window (top). She gathered up her children's favorite clothes and possessions (above).

Along with the necessities for herself, Rosalyn grabbed a statue from a beauty contest she'd won in 1971 (above) and loaded everything into a van for a quick getaway (top). Rosalyn says she now has a productive life that includes being a part of the campaign to end violence against women.

Jenny was feeling shaky about herself before she met Cal. Surgery had left her with scars on her belly. She felt unattractive and vulnerable, but Cal made her feel wanted. He was very tender when they made love. He didn't lay a violent hand on her until she moved in with him.

During the next three years, Cal broke Jenny's nose—"He accused me of doing something with another man," she says. He broke one of her fingers with a hockey stick—"I came home late." He punched her mouth and knocked a tooth out—"He said I made his car malfunction." He cut her ear with a pair of scissors—"He wasn't sexually satisfied." He dominated her completely, forbidding her to see any friends, telling her when she could eat, sleep, watch TV, go to the bathroom, and leave the house.

They were married in 1985. Jenny says, "I was really scared that if I told him I wouldn't marry him, then he wouldn't believe I loved him, and that would have led to a fight, and I might have been dead by now."

Gradually Jenny became more withdrawn, rarely smiling or looking at anyone but Cal, for fear of setting him off. But her docile behavior didn't stop Cal's violence. She was afraid to strike back and too terrified to leave. (In fact, an abuser is most likely to attack and kill when a woman attempts to get away.) But in October, when Cal threatened to kill Jenny and brought a heavy ashtray down on her head, she moved out.

A month later, a judge signed a temporary restraining order for Jenny. The order was good for one week; then Cal was due to appear for a hearing. The judge wanted to hear his side of the story before issuing a yearlong protection order. Jenny went back to her old house, with police backup standing across the street, and personally handed Cal the papers summoning him to appear. He didn't show up in court. A contempt charge was filed, but he was never picked up. Jenny hadn't realized that domestic abuse warrants were not followed up in Philadelphia.

While Cal was free, Jenny lived in a women's shelter. When her thirty days there were up, the advocates at the shelter helped her find a place to live. She filed divorce papers. Feeling like a new woman, Jenny found a good job and earned a promotion within weeks. It seemed that she was finally gaining control of her life.

Then, without warning, Cal tracked her down. Late one night in March, as Jenny sat watching TV with a girlfriend, Cal broke down her door. He had a .357 Magnum wrapped in white tape tucked inside his pants. He grabbed for her, and she ran to the phone, but he pulled the wires out of the wall. Her neighbor ran downstairs to call the police. Cal pulled Jenny onto the living room sofa and took out his gun. He told her it was time to die. But within five minutes of his entry, the police were climbing the stairs. When they came in with guns drawn, Cal rammed his weapon between the sofa cushions. He told them Jenny was his wife, as though that explained everything. But this time, the police took him in.

Cal was charged with six offenses, including criminal trespass, simple assault, and possession of an instrument of crime. Jenny assumed that Cal would be put away for a while, perhaps until the preliminary hearing in Municipal Court. But she was wrong. He went free the next morning. Bail had been set at $2,500, so Cal bought quick freedom for $250.

When Jenny heard that Cal was free again, she fled back to the shelter. She felt it was a giant step backward. With help from Women Against Abuse and the district attorney, she located Cal's probation officer and told him that Cal had failed to appear in Family Court, in violation of his parole. When Cal went for a routine visit with his parole officer, the sheriff arrested him. A detainer charge from the parole officer kept Cal in jail until his felony trial.

Cal's lawyer, Joseph Santaguida, said, "Did Cal ever smack her? I don't know. Everyone gets mad sometimes, pushes a woman a little." Cal was convicted on all counts except burglary. The judge was not moved when Cal described himself as a man whose heart had been broken.

After the trial, Jenny said, "I'm tired of running. Why should I have to run and hide? Why can't I live here without hiding? . . . Please, I just want this to be over with. . . . At least now I know where he's at. And you know what else? If he's in for a while, maybe it'll help him straighten out. Maybe I'm helping to save his life."

Jenny complained to a Family Court officer that her husband "violated his parole a thousand ways, not including what he's done to me."

Her husband always threatened to kill Jenny if she ever left him. She believed he'd do it, but the day came when she decided she had no choice. A shelter gave Jenny security while each day she went out to search for a job and an apartment, bundled up in various disguises. To strengthen her case against Cal, Jenny looked for evidence of his law-breaking. She dug through city-hall records looking for evidence of bigamy. Although there was none, the act itself was important. She was learning to take power.

Jenny asked for a police escort to deliver a court summons to her husband, but the officers refused and waited for her across the street. Standing at the door of her former home (top left) and sounding braver than she felt, Jenny told Cal, "Make sure you're there." He never showed up. Jenny (bottom left) worked hard at making a better life than she'd had with Cal. She found a job with a large real-estate company. She was quickly promoted. Cal (below) was eventually convicted of assaulting her.

JANICE'S STORY

It was the spring of 1984 when I first met Janice at a safe house. She was always sitting alone, smoking cigarettes, never talking to anyone. She seemed locked inside herself. The safe house director, Joan Welsh, explained that Janice was part of the California Witness Protection Program—she had come to them through the underground shelter system. They knew she had witnessed a murder, that she had been battered, and that she was pregnant, but her full story was still a mystery.

I asked Janice if it would help her to talk, and she told me about her life. Like so many abused women, Janice had done everything she could to change her situation: she worked hard, she sought and followed advice, she took risks to find a way out. Nonetheless, Janice felt she was somehow responsible for the tragedies in her life.

For five years, Janice had been living with R.J., a violent man with a large gun collection who was in the habit of shooting so as just to miss her. He drank and used drugs. He lost his job, and his violent behavior worsened. He frequently threatened to kill Janice or one of their children if she tried to leave. Janice prayed for a miracle to help her escape from that hell.

"I was crazy to put up with it," she says, "but I was always told, 'If you leave me, I'll kill you.' . . . That's why I stayed."

Eventually, though, Janice took the children and moved in with her mother and stepfather. But R.J.'s abusive behavior continued.

One night he came to my parents' house after everybody went to sleep. He started to go through my bag, tearing things up. Suddenly, he was standing over me with a Vick's jar. He slammed it into my eye. I started screaming for help, and I tried to get into the bathroom, but R.J. kept pushing me down. My hands were leaving blood prints over the walls. I tried to dial 911, but the blood covered the phone. The woman upstairs had heard me screaming and she'd already called. When the police came, they handcuffed R.J. immediately. . . .

The next day was the first time I checked into a battered-women's shelter. When I got there, I thought, "What am I going to do?" They kept telling me, "You have to be out of here in six weeks. Do you want to get an apartment?" But I couldn't do it on my own.

At the shelter, Janice met Kim, who helped her to find an apartment. By December, Janice was set up in a nice place with her children, and she and Kim had become good friends. They found strength in their similarities. They were neighbors, each of them had a son and a daughter; they wore the same dress size, and they were born the same month of the same year. And they both had violent husbands threatening their sanity and security.

On December 31st everything went wrong.

We'd been living in Pittsburg [California] for less than a month, but everything was going good. We had jobs and new boyfriends. I got my kids dressed, grabbed a bag of clothes, and went over to Kim's house. Somebody knocked on the door. It was her husband, Gabe. He said, "I'm hungry and I don't have any money." First Kim said, "I don't have any food," but then she felt sorry for him. "Okay, Gabe, you can have a sandwich. But you have to hurry up." He came in saying hi to everyone, in a good mood. He fixed a sandwich and had a soda. But their son saw him take a knife from the drawer. Gabe told the boy, "If you tell your mom I've got this knife, I'll kill her."

So as we walked along to the bus stop, the child knew his dad had the knife, but he was scared to tell. At the bus stop everything was fine. The bus arrived. I turned to tell the kids and Kim to get ready. Then I saw Gabe holding Kim like he was embracing her—but he was stabbing her. She was turning and twisting every which way to escape his knife plunging into her chest. I tried to pull him off. Before he'd finished, he had stabbed her seventeen times. Then he just dropped her in the gutter. I held her in my arms and watched him run away. He dropped the knife in the grass and turned around once to say, "I hope she's dead."

After Kim's death, Janice began to feel paranoid. "I had this fear about leaving my house," she reports. "When I tried to go out I'd reach for the doorknob, but I couldn't open it. Then, the first night I go out to dinner, I try to get into my car and I find a man leaning over it, shot in the back. I looked at it like an omen: Is this where R.J. is going to find me? Everything began to look like a warning."

The people at the shelter where Janice had stayed shared her fears. They were determined that what

When she thought she had escaped violence, Janice witnessed the murder of her friend, Kim, whose husband killed her at the bus stop.

had happened to Kim would not happen to Janice and her children. R.J. was becoming more and more threatening: he told the child protective authorities that he would kill Janice if he was not allowed to see his children. The authorities advised Janice to leave her home and go underground. When she refused to take this step, they took her children away.

"At first I was fighting them," she says. "I wasn't doing anything wrong—they had to give me back my kids. Then I just totally gave up. I called the lady and said, 'Okay, I'm leaving. I'll have everything ready.' I gave away all my stuff and went into the shelter. The next week they gave me my kids." She and her children were moved to a shelter in another part of the country, where they lived unhappily, confined and estranged.

"It's just a matter of time before I lose what little hold on myself I have," she told me. "What's the point in me being in a battered-women's shelter? I got out of that life. I got away from that man. I had really high hopes of getting help. But . . . who gives a shit? Nobody. I am still in hell."

Janice sobbed in court, struggling to tell how she'd seen Gabe murder her best friend, Kim, his estranged wife (above). A bus driver testified he'd also seen the killing (top). "It looks like a domestic," the driver had shouted to his passengers. He said he'd locked the doors and blown the horn.

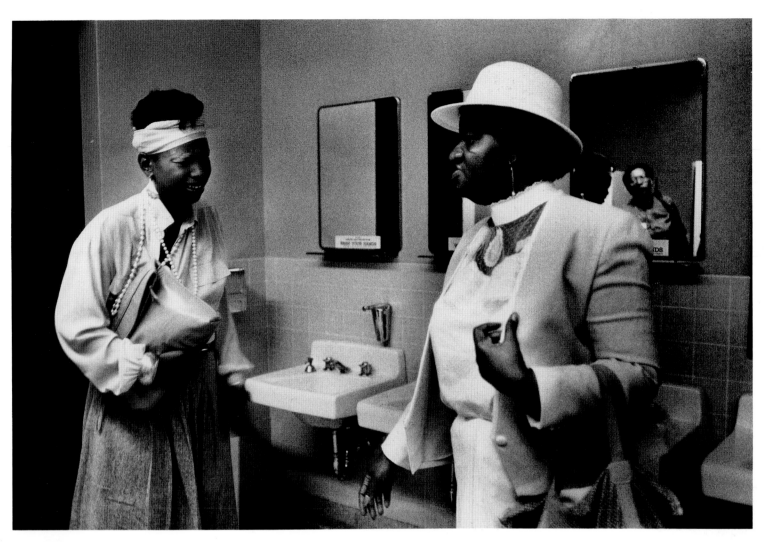

Kim's mother (top) and friends (above) tried to comfort Janice. Kim was stabbed seventeen times and died in Janice's arms. Although Gabe had obviously planned the murder, the jury called it an unpremeditated crime of passion. Gabe (overleaf) was paroled after less than four years in prison.

CHARLOTTE'S STORY

As Charlotte Fedders listened to Ronald Reagan deliver his 1984 State of the Union speech, in which he promised to devote his efforts to stopping "horrible crimes like sexual abuse and family violence," she thought to herself, "Perhaps President Reagan could do something to stop my husband from hitting me." So she wrote a letter to the president detailing her difficulties in trying to stay alive. She lost her nerve and never mailed it, but her sister mailed it for her. A year later, Charlotte sat in a courtroom in Maryland, telling the story of her life with the man who'd terrified her for fifteen years.

On February 27, 1985, the *Wall Street Journal* reported Charlotte's story. On the same day, her husband, John Fedders, chief law-enforcement officer of the Securities and Exchange Commission in the Reagan Administration, resigned from his post.

Fedders admitted to beating his wife fifteen times. In court he said, "There was no justification for hitting Charlotte. . . . I am forever remorseful about it. . . . Yes, I demeaned her. I did a lot of stupid things."

His admission caused a major crack in the armor that shielded Washington society from life's realities. No one could comprehend how this successful man could go home and batter his wife. The press cornered Charlotte, and pummeled her with accusative questions. She was forced to explain again and again why she had stayed so long with such a man.

First of all, she explained, she tried everything to save their marriage because she believed that marriage vows are sacred. Secondly, she always found a way to excuse her husband's actions. When he got angry, she truly believed she must have done something wrong. Charlotte had grown up the model Catholic girl. In her book, *Shattered Dreams*, written after her divorce, she says, "Until my marriage broke up, I honestly believed that if I was good, prayed, went to confession and to church, obeyed the Ten Commandments, and devoted myself to my loved ones that nothing bad could happen to me. I was convinced that bad things only came as a punishment for some fault in me."

So when Charlotte and John Fedders were still newlyweds and the six-foot-six-inch John hit her hard enough to break her eardrum, she felt more confusion and shame than pain. "My intelligence kept telling me that I had done nothing wrong, but my heart kept saying I must have. Why else would he have done it?"

"My father told me to get out while I could," says Charlotte, "before I had children. But I just couldn't leave John. I loved him. And I thought the ultimate disgrace was a failed marriage . . . the Church said divorce was a sin."

The beatings escalated over the years. She stopped telling her parents about the problem because she had made up her mind to make the best of her marriage. She says, "It became my own horrible secret."

Eventually, though, in February 1983, Charlotte wrote a letter to her husband asking for a divorce. "As much as I love you—and I do—I have finally learned to love myself. . . . Why didn't you believe me when I said I would never let you do that to me again? . . . No woman deserves to be beaten by her husband, not ever. . . . The final realization is that you are incapable of showing me and my children the respect and . . . love that we deserve. . . . I can no longer have you living in the same house as the boys and me."

In *Shattered Dreams*, Charlotte writes of her determination to leave behind the oppressive notions of womanhood that she had been programmed to accept and to value. From a strict Catholic girl, Charlotte became an outspoken woman fighting for every woman's right to life without fear.

Shattered Dreams was a well-thumbed book on my bookshelf when Dick Polman, a reporter with whom I had collaborated in the past, called to see if I wanted to photograph Charlotte Fedders. A court master had just ruled that John Fedders was entitled to receive twenty-five percent of the book's royalties. The logic was that because of Fedders's participation in the story, he was entitled to payment. As Mary McGrory wrote in the *Washington Post*, "By that standard, Adolf Hitler, had he lived, would have had a share in the proceeds from *The Diary of Anne Frank* . . . if Hitler had not ordered the extermination of the Jews, she would not have had the material for her masterpiece." On February 10, 1988, Polman reported in the *Philadelphia Inquirer* that a Maryland judge had overturned the ruling, saying that the fault for the breakup was John's—that he shouldn't have hit her, no matter what reason he gave.

Today Charlotte Fedders lives in a small house. She is struggling to pay the bills for herself and her four children on her salary from the flower shop where she works. But she has a sense of her own strength, and the conviction that she will never again have to live like a prisoner in her own home.

Charlotte, wife of a top government official, sued for divorce charging physical cruelty, puncturing the myth that only the poor get battered.

SANDRA'S STORY

The *Philadelphia Inquirer Sunday Magazine* commissioned reporter Dick Polman and me to do a story on domestic violence in Philadelphia. We found that getting the firsthand stories of battered women presented a number of serious difficulties, as well as some ethical problems.

Living in shelters was one way to meet battered women. Visiting hospital emergency rooms was another, but my presence there created an understandable dilemma for the hospital staff. They felt it was unprofessional to ask a badly injured battered woman whether a photographer could come talk with her. That was the hardest part—asking permission to invade the privacy of a patient at what might be one of the worst moments of her life. Most of the time I got what I expected—rejection. Then I met Sandra.

It was just after 11:00 one night in December 1987. Jay McInerney, the emergency-room night manager at Albert Einstein hospital, who had been trained to work with battered women, suggested I approach two women in the examination room and try to find out what had happened.

Opening the door, I saw a brown-skinned woman holding a tiny baby in her arms. She sat motionless on an operating table. Next to her was another woman, stiffly holding up her hand, her face contorted in pain. Dashing in circles around them was an excited little girl.

I introduced myself, explaining that I was doing an article about domestic violence. I asked if what they had been through might have anything to do with my story, and both women nodded. Then I asked them if I could photograph whatever happened to them from that point onward, to which they agreed. As the hours passed, various doctors came in to examine and treat Sandra and the woman who had saved her life, Lily.

On Friday night, forty-eight hours before, Sandra's husband Terry had come home in a nasty mood. When little Marie saw her father's expression, she asked, "Daddy, are you going to hurt Mommy again?" He locked Marie in the closet and chased Sandra into the basement, where he tore off most of her clothes and began beating her, smashing heavy objects into her face and pounding her head into the wall. The beating continued into Sunday. That night, in desperation, Sandra broke the lock on the basement door and ran out across the backyards, knocking on back doors, crying for help. It was pitch dark and cold, and Sandra was barefoot and half-dressed. No one even turned on their porch lights. When she came to Lily's house, the door opened, and Lily brought Sandra in and found her a pair of boots and a sweater. Shivering from the cold and the pain, Sandra told her what had happened. And she said that her children were trapped with Terry in the house, and she was desperate to get them out. Lily agreed to help. Lily's sister Luna was reluctant about the rescue mission, but she would not let them go alone.

So the three women went to Sandra's house together. The first thing Lily saw was long clumps of black hair on the rug—Sandra's hair. Terry came down the stairs and started toward Sandra, who grabbed the baby and fled through the front door. Lily glared at Terry and said, "Is that what a big man you are, beating up on women?" He punched her in the face. She and Luna ran out of the house with Terry right behind them. Sandra hid behind a tree. It was pitch dark. Terry took out a knife and stabbed Lily's hand. She screamed when she saw the blood. One of the neighbors called the police; when they finally arrived, they checked the women's injuries. They allowed Terry to go back inside the house.

The police followed Lily's car as she drove over to the hospital with Sandra, Luna, and the children. As Lily waited for a doctor to repair the tendon in her right hand, she warned Sandra against returning home. "Don't ever go back," she said, "because they keep on doing it. You shouldn't have to take that from anybody; that's not what love's all about."

Sandra mulled over Lily's advice, but she was still holding on to a hope that her husband might change. A month later Sandra took Terry back, but she warned him that she still intended to testify against him at the misdemeanor trial. She hoped that would make him change his ways. But shortly before the trial was to take place, Terry was found dead behind the wheel of his car on the highway. His death

Months after her husband died, Sandra searched in vain for his grave. She said, "I could never find Terry when he was alive, either."

certificate read: "accidental overdose of drugs and alcohol."

Spring came, and Dick Polman and I went back to visit Sandra. She was feeling ready to visit Terry's grave for the first time since the funeral.

On the way to the cemetery she told us about her marriage. Sandra had met Terry when she was seventeen years old. He was a U.S. serviceman; she was a girl from Fiji who still lived with her parents. He pursued her and she fell in love. They got married and moved to Philadelphia, where Terry had family. They had children, two girls. "All I ever wanted to do was to make everyone happy," Sandra said. "But sometimes I don't know what love is about. . . . I loved him for his good side. For the bad side, I sometimes felt like killing him." She described what had bound her to Terry until his death: "I was scared of being on my own. And I thought I could help him."

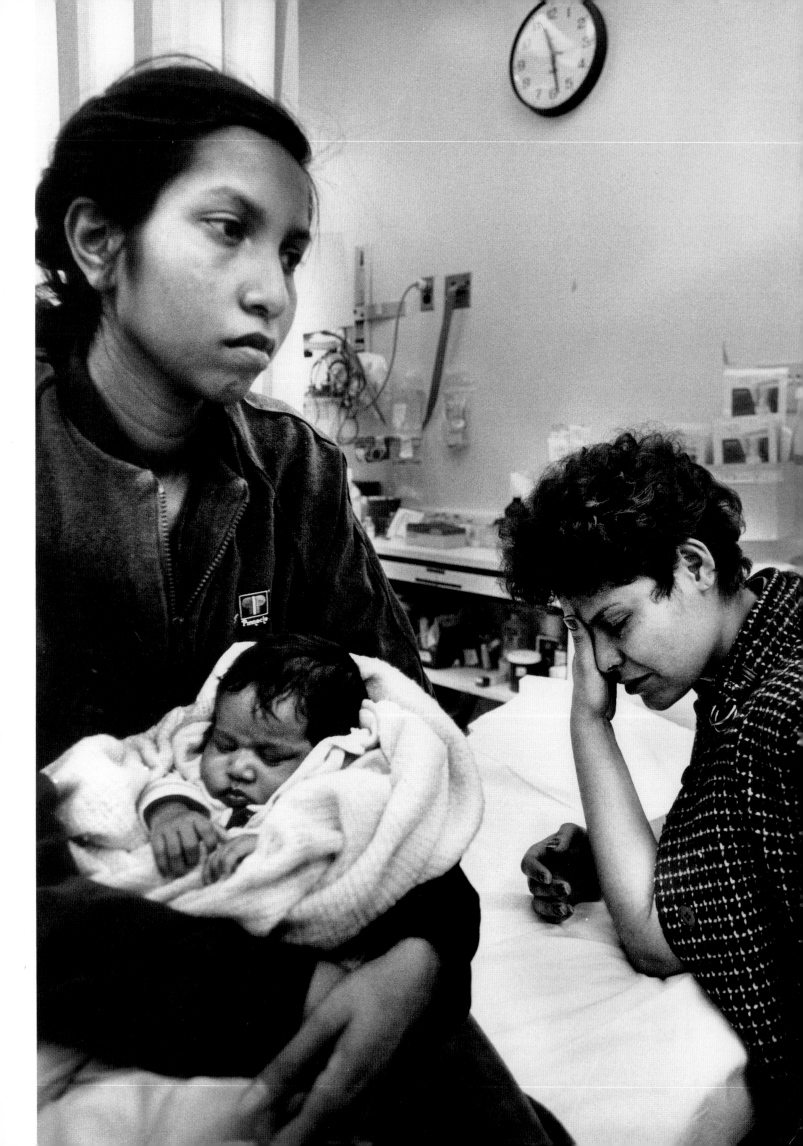

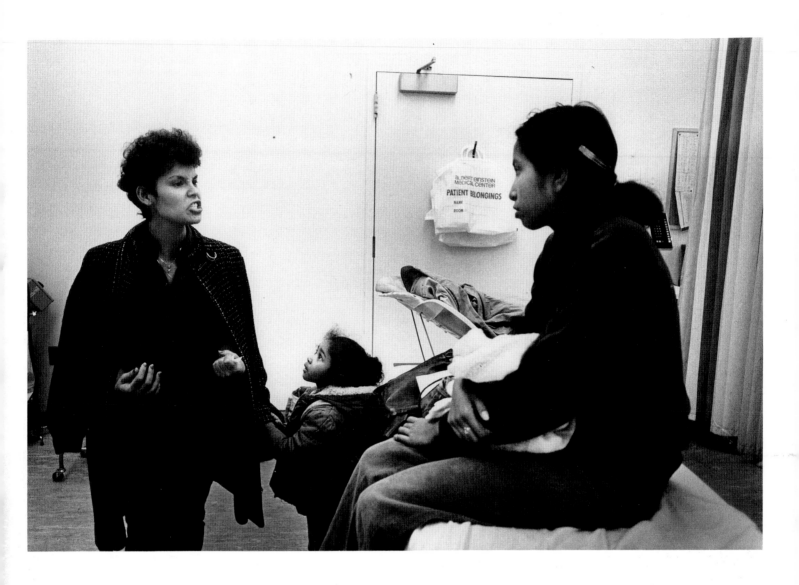

Helping women in need isn't always convenient or even
safe, but some women are willing to take the risks because
they know it's necessary. When Sandra came to Lily's
house, Lily knew she couldn't shut the door. They returned to
Sandra's house to rescue her children. The husband, Terry,
attacked Lily. While both women were being treated in the
hospital emergency room (left), Lily told Sandra she had to
stay away from Terry. "If you don't go back," she argued
(above), "everything I've suffered tonight will be worth it."

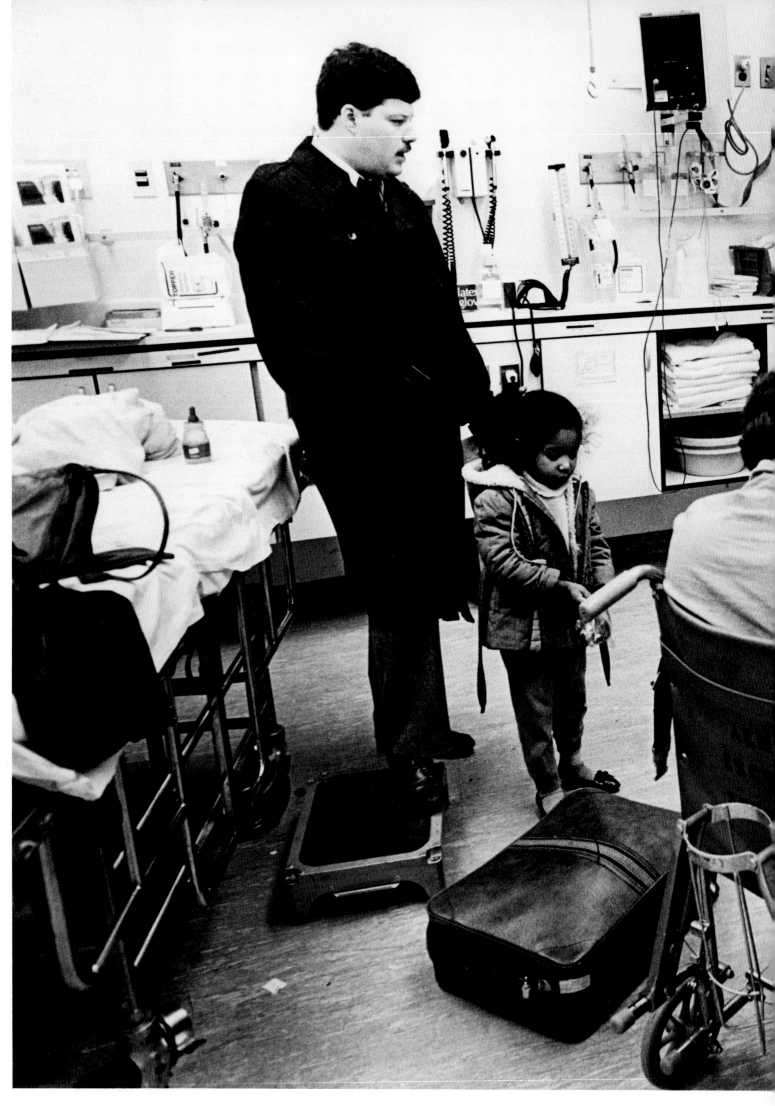

Sandra slept in a hospital office after being treated. The next morning she and her daughters went to a shelter where they stayed for a few weeks.

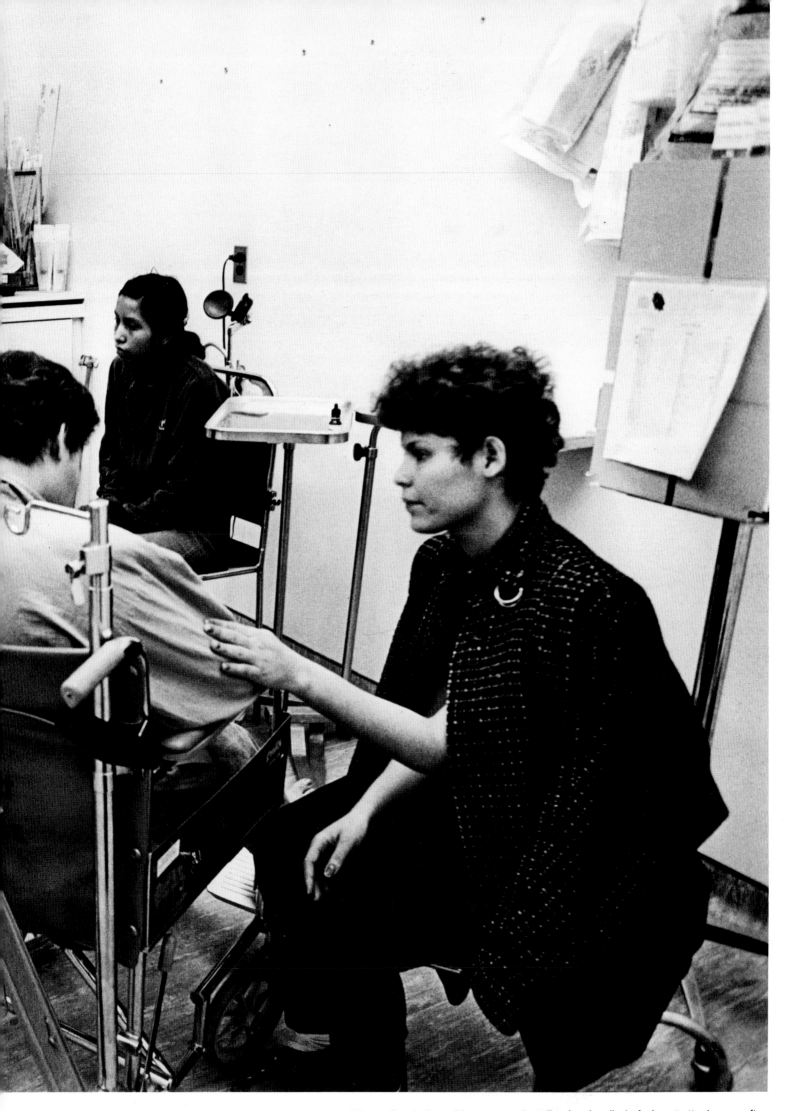

Having no place else to go, they returned to their home —and Terry. Sandra's problems were short-lived —he died of a heart attack soon after.

Tuesday morning, November 3, 1987, the headlines of a *Newsday* story tucked in the middle of the paper read, "Girl, 6, Is Critically Injured. Parents Are Arrested, Charged." It was the day after Lisa Steinberg had been found unconscious in a Greenwich Village apartment. "The wife also appears to have been beaten," Aaron Rosenthal, Assistant Chief of the Manhattan Detective Borough, told the press. Hedda Nussbaum had a bandaged nose, puffy eyes, and bruises on her head and body. The accompanying photograph depicted her looking downward, her lips split like a boxer's, her nose broken, strands of wild gray hair escaping from a dirty bandanna. Next to her was a strong-looking, full-chested, confident man: Joel Steinberg.

On the following day, front-page headlines read, "Sleeping Beauty—Six Years Old—Extremely Critical, May Be Declared Brain Dead." The third page carried an interview with a fifteen-year-old girl named Amanda Willhelm, a neighbor, who said that until a year ago, Lisa had seemed like a cheery and healthy girl. But in recent months, she had been seen with scrapes and black-and-blue marks, a hunk of her hair hacked off, and a big bruise on her side. The teenager reported that Lisa had said that her baby brother did these things. Amanda's family suspected Lisa was being abused, but they said nothing because they were afraid Steinberg might take it out on Lisa if they went to the authorities.

Amanda described Steinberg as "a big, great influential person . . . he just seemed very hard." This may have been the way that two unwed teenaged mothers saw Steinberg, the "adoption" lawyer, when they handed over their babies to him—ostensibly for him to place in good homes. Instead, Steinberg kept the babies and called them Lisa and Mitchell Steinberg.

Lisa's natural mother, Michele Launders, had been an easy target for a forceful lawyer with no scruples. Not only did Steinberg take her baby, but he also took a $500 fee to place her baby girl in a "proper Christian home." Steinberg was an expert at taking advantage of people's weaknesses and misfortunes.

While argument raged in the press about the case, many commentators overlooked that Hedda Nussbaum, Steinberg's companion, was obviously a bat-

tered woman. Having spent a good deal of time as an observer in battered-women's shelters over the last six years, I recognized the dazed, debilitated look that Hedda wore in the news photos.

I went to see Hedda's attorney, Barry Scheck, to offer my pictures of battered women, thinking they might help her to see that she was not alone. Scheck pulled out an envelope with hospital pictures of Hedda taken on the night of November 3. They looked like photographs of a war victim. On one leg she had an infected ulceration. Her ear was swollen and misshapen. Her head appeared to have been punched in at the sides. Her skin was scarred by cigarette burns. There was absolutely nothing human in her expression: no shame, no embarrassment, no suffering. She was more dead than anything else. I studied those photographs and thought about people who say that women stay with violent men because they like it.

When Steinberg went on trial for Lisa's murder, I began working on a story about Hedda for *People*. Naomi Weiss, an old friend of Hedda's, was the writer. Over three weekends in December 1988, I visited Hedda on the snowy grounds of Four Winds hospital where she was undergoing intensive psychotherapy. Although I was there to photograph, mostly we talked. Hedda was stronger physically and mentally than I had expected, owing to a year of hospitalization under the care of Dr. Samuel Klagsbrun.

As we talked, I began to understand that Hedda had endured years of physical torture, preceded by years of skillful psychological abuse and mental attrition. By the time Steinberg first hit her, he had already convinced Hedda that she deserved it. After a while, she could find no escape and no help. She became a living corpse.

Hedda told me that she had never seen Steinberg hit Lisa, and that, although he had battered Hedda regularly, until the last year, he had shown great pride in Lisa. But the downward spiral in Lisa's relationship with Steinberg was swift. Lisa's terror must have been paralyzing, because she knew the violence he was capable of; she had spent years trying to distract the man she called Dad from beating the woman she called Mom.

"One of the ways Joel would punish me," Hedda said, "was to force me to lie in the bathtub filled with

Hedda Nussbaum survived the extreme physical and mental brutality of Joel Steinberg, but their little "adopted" daughter Lisa did not.

freezing cold water. Joel made Lisa watch as he hit me and listen as he explained, 'Daddy's helping Mommy.' Sometimes he would ask Lisa if he should hit me. If Lisa would say no, he would definitely hit me, explaining why I needed to be punished. So Lisa tried to say 'yes' once, thinking that he would go the opposite way and not hit me. Of course, it didn't matter. I still got hit."

Hedda's testimony was vital to Steinberg's prosecution, yet many jurors and journalists blamed her for failing to save Lisa's life. Some blamed her for the murder. In the end, the jury found Steinberg guilty only of manslaughter.

Like so many batterers, Steinberg continues to deny any responsibility for his actions. On December 5, 1990, when *Newsday* columnist Carole Agus asked Steinberg about his relationship with Hedda, he maintained, "We didn't have a violent relationship. In fact, there was no violence in our relationship at all."

Today Hedda lives alone in a small secluded house, cut off from everyone she loved. Her financial situation is precarious; often she turns to temporary secretarial agencies for work. She continues to attend battered-women's meetings.

Under pressure from Joel Steinberg, Hedda Nussbaum had lost contact with her parents. At the hospital where Nussbaum recovered from Joel Steinberg's horrific abuse, her elderly parents, Willy and Emma (above), talked about the night they learned of Lisa's death and Hedda's battered condition. As Emma recalled, "First I got this telephone call from Charlotte, Joel's mother. She was upset. 'Did you see the six o'clock news, Emma? They say a little girl named Lisa has been found badly beaten.' 'Well, there are lots of Lisas in the world, Charlotte,' I said. 'No, no. They say she lived on 12th Street and her father was a lawyer, and they are bringing him into custody.' Well, I started to get worried, too, so I telephoned Hedda's apartment. But there was no answer. I called everywhere, but I couldn't find Hedda. Then I sat down and wrote her a long letter about all the things I'd been worried about for so many years. I mailed it that night, but she never got it." Then Willy interjected, "We were calling all over the city trying to find Hedda and Lisa." Touching Hedda's cheek, he said, "For a while we thought we'd lost them until we realized that we were the ones who'd been lost from Hedda."

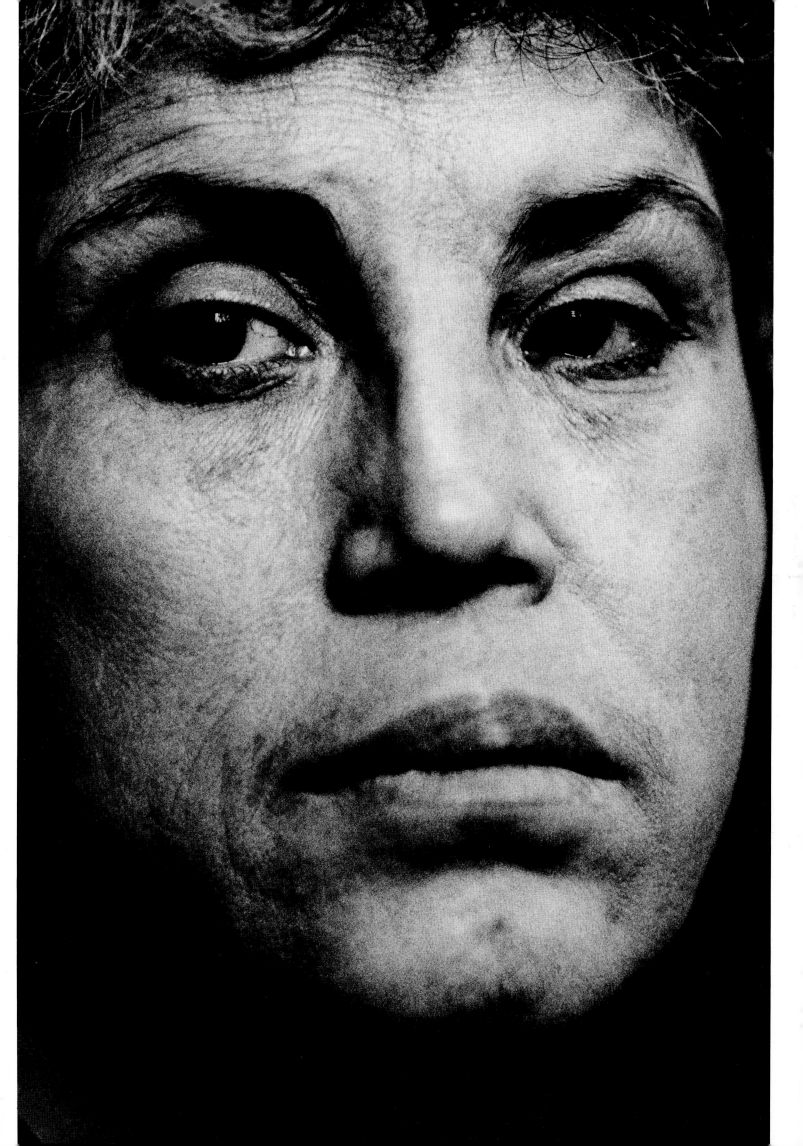

LISA AND GARTH'S STORY

In 1981 I was assigned by Japanese Playboy to photograph couples who epitomized the glamorous life-styles of that era. I couldn't have found a better example than Lisa and Garth, a striking couple I'd met while doing a story on New York nightlife.

Garth was a very successful engineer and designer: a self-made man. Lisa, his stunning wife, mother of five, was the envy of everyone who knew them. Garth had designed their eight-bedroom mansion with Jacuzzi and sauna, a swimming pool off the master bedroom, and a high-tech camera/intercom system set up to monitor family activities in each room of the house. The estate was protected by white hunting dogs that prowled the grounds sniffing for trespassers. These were privileged people with all the happiness money could buy.

Because I was attempting to show the way the couple's social life meshed with their family life, I had to spend a fair amount of time at this home in Westchester. Over the course of a year, I spent many nights and days with them, observing wild parties as well as private family moments. No one ever seemed uncomfortable with my camera. A sense of trust and ease was quickly established.

However, the more I watched this family, the more I had the sense that, in fact, all was not well. There were underlying tensions that at first surfaced only occasionally. When I found that their freewheeling activities included cocaine, the problems became more visible. I was photographing a family living under incredible stress.

Garth would force Lisa to behave in ways she didn't like. "Sometimes I get angry with him for encouraging me to do things which are too sensational," she told me. "Yet he says that he does it entirely for my sake, that he doesn't want me to change who I am no matter where I am or who I am with. He says he is pushing me to realize my fullest potential."

To Garth, Lisa's "potential" meant what she could do for his business and personal reputation. He exploited her physical beauty as well as her nurturing instincts. After their third child was born, Lisa was not as interested in nightlife. But Garth relentlessly insisted that they stay out late, and that she have sex with his friends, promising that once the fun was over, she could go home to the children.

My diary describes their family life as I watched it rapidly degenerating:

—Thursday night, December 31, 1981

Garth and Lisa's New Year's Eve party. Wild beyond words. Men whose last names end in "o" work in the kitchen, fry sausage and peppers, stir the spaghetti sauce, count little white bags in the bedroom. Friends of Lisa's teenage daughter Jean get bombed at the party, which turns into an orgy. With no supervision, the rowdy kids punch holes in walls and break most of Lisa's best crystal. Disco music blasts till dawn.

—Friday night, January 1, 1982

Endless arguments break out between Garth and Lisa. Frustrated from little sleep or food, excessive amounts of alcohol, drugs, and her husband's paranoia, Lisa cries and cries that she doesn't know why she is no longer interested in having sex with him.

When I had a baby in February, I fell out of touch with Lisa and Garth for a few months. Upon returning to Westchester, I found the tension in the house unbearable.

—Thursday morning, May 6

Lisa looks haunted. Garth is stretched out like a skeleton. His eyes are shadows of the past. The sound of a feather landing would make him jump. He lives on English muffins and coffee, but only Lisa is allowed to serve him. As parents they are emotionally absent.

—Friday night, May 7

My baby and I are sleeping in the Blue Room. Suddenly the sounds of shouting and things breaking come from the master bedroom. I take my camera and venture down the hall to find out what is wrong. Garth is in a rage, pulling everything from the closet shelves, shouting at Lisa as if she were a child. I start photographing, not knowing what's going to happen. But I am scared.

When I first saw Garth hit Lisa, I couldn't believe my eyes. Instinctively, I took a picture. But when he went to hit her again, I grabbed his arm and pleaded with him to stop. He hardly noticed my presence, nor did he seem to care that anyone was watching. This surprised me at the time. Now, nine years later, I know that when a man is determined to beat his wife, he will do it in front of the children, or the neighbors, or even the police.

Garth's response to my plea was, "I know my own strength. And I'm not going to hurt her. I'm only going to teach her a lesson."

Summoning up her courage, Lisa had hidden Garth's cocaine pipe, believing that it was the root of their problems. Although he had several other pipes, Garth was making his point that she could not act without his approval. Until then she'd always been "the obedient wife." This was the first time she had gone against him. Lisa was distraught. I stayed with her as she cried, saying, "I always thought he loved me, but tonight he beat me like he wouldn't touch the dog. I'll never again believe in his love."

When I left the next day I thought they were completely mad. Nothing made sense. At home I threw the roll of film into a drawer and, because I didn't know how to respond to the events of that night, I tried to forget the whole episode. As the months went by, I tried to convince myself it had never happened. (I know now that my denial of the seriousness of what I had witnessed and my effort to overlook it are typical responses to domestic

Lisa and Garth gave the appearance of being a liberated, happy couple, but Garth's violence was slowly destroying his wife and family.

violence. Family members, friends, neighbors, doctors, police, judges—all often react in just that way.)

Eventually, however, curiosity took over and I called their home. Garth answered and told me that he had just admitted Lisa to a detox center for her drinking problem. "What about you?" I asked. "Oh no, I'm fine. I have everything under control. But Lisa is in very bad shape."

Lisa had told me about some strange incidents that seemed to indicate that Garth was playing games with her mind. Once, she returned home from grocery shopping to find her suitcases lined up in the hallway. "You're going on a trip," Garth told her. "I didn't know that," Lisa said. And then, just as suddenly, the suitcases disappeared. On another occasion, Lisa returned home and found Garth lying in a pool of blood on the shower floor. Screaming, she ran to the phone to call the police. When she hung up, Garth stood beside her, dripping water, but otherwise alive and well. "Is anything wrong, dear?" he asked calmly.

With these troubling incidents in mind, I decided to go see Lisa in the detox center. Garth was there. The sight of him and of her black eye were not encouraging. As she drank coffee from a plastic mug, I asked how she'd gotten the shiner. Garth wrapped his arm tightly around her shoulders. "I must have been drunk and fallen," Lisa said. "I must have hit my head against the coffee table."

This time, I knew better.

I went home, took the roll of film from the drawer, and went into the darkroom. The evidence became clear: the black-and-white frames showed a man beating his wife. I felt powerless. I wanted to call them and say, "Look, you need help," but I felt it was not my place. The worst part was realizing that I had been trying to ignore the truth of what I'd seen.

In time, Lisa's bruises went away. She returned home from the detox center to find long-stemmed red roses awaiting her in every room. Banners declaring Garth's eternal love were hung on the walls. He bought her extravagant presents. It seemed like the honeymoon was just beginning. But soon enough, the abuse began again, even more brutally than before. A couple of months later, Garth beat Lisa and jumped up and down on her crumpled body. Their eldest son called the police, and Garth was taken to jail.

Lisa hired a lawyer who helped her obtain a restraining order. Garth was not allowed to go near the house. Soon after, Lisa divorced him, gave the house back to Garth, and moved away with her children to a more modest home. Garth does not provide child support. Lisa is completely responsible for herself and her children.

Garth lingered on in the mansion with a pet boa constrictor and a pet ferret, kept in adjacent glass boxes. The ferret was forced to live in a state of constant anxiety next to the eye of the ever-hungry snake. To this day, Garth denies ever hitting Lisa.

Early in the day, Garth tried to drag Lisa into the house because he couldn't find his cocaine pipe. Their three-year-old son cried so hysterically

that Garth let go of Lisa. He returned to his bedroom and stayed there brooding for the rest of the day. Later, his brooding turned to violence.

During the middle of the night, Garth cornered Lisa in their bathroom, still hunting for his cocaine pipe (top). "I've hidden it," she said, "to save our marriage." "You're lying, you wanted it for yourself," Garth shouted. He grabbed one of Lisa's fur coats and threatened to burn it (above).

He ransacked the bathroom searching frantically for the pipe (top). Suddenly he hit Lisa (above). Garth raged and threw Lisa on the marble counter (overleaf). When he finally found the pipe, he smashed it. "I had my own all the time," he said smugly. "I just wanted to teach you a lesson."

Garth checked Lisa into a detox center (above) because he said alcohol was ruining her. When she returned home from the center, Garth entered what some psychologists call "the honeymoon phase." He heaped expensive presents on Lisa. He strung banners around the house declaring himself her "loving husband" (above right) and filled every room with long-stemmed red roses. The "honeymoon" didn't last long. His violence became worse than ever. During his last attack, Garth bit one of Lisa's fingers, dragged her up and down the stairs until she bled, and then jumped up and down on her body. Lisa shouted, "Garth, remember it's me! Stop, it's Lisa." He raped her and threw her outside naked. Their young son called the police.

LISA
I LOVE YOU, AND I
WILL DO SO FOREVER.
I AM SO HAPPY THAT
YOU ARE BACK HOME.
YOUR HUSBAND

Lisa divorced Garth. Through the help of friends during the transitional period, and after a long time studying to be a reflexologist and shiatsu practitioner, Lisa finally was able to bring a sense of order back into her family life. Garth (above) kept his boa constrictor and ferret in the same bathroom where he had beaten Lisa.

BECCA'S STORY

In a maximum-security prison, Becca Jean Hughes, 41, told me her story. "Don's hands had closed down on my windpipe. He had been beating me all the way home till he pulled off on a dirt road in the snow. The last thing I ever told him was that I was going to leave him. The last thing he said was that I was a bad bitch."

As she struggled for her life, Becca's fingers found the .22 revolver Don kept under the driver's seat. She held it out so Don could see it, but his hands stayed firmly around her neck. Becca hesitated, "He didn't give me permission to shoot him, and God forbid, I thought I needed that. It was like I couldn't function without his permission. I almost let that man choke me to death before I pulled the trigger."

She continued, "How many times had this man told me I was dead? But when he said he was going for the kids after he killed me, I don't know . . . but I couldn't let him do it to them. I pulled the trigger and fired at the floor. Don never went for the gun. Then I shot him. He never said, 'Don't shoot'—I don't think he believed that I'd shoot him. I didn't know I shot him. I just kept shooting, even when the gun was empty."

On May 16, 1985, Becca, a half-blooded Cherokee mother of seven children, was found guilty of first-degree murder and sentenced to fifty years imprisonment with no parole. (The average murderer in America serves only six years.)

Five years later, when we talked in the prison, Becca told me that Don wasn't the only man to abuse her. Her father beat her, and her first husband was also violent.

Becca said that during their first eight years together, Don "never raised his voice, never swatted me, never slapped a child. He was the type of husband you would have given a medal to. But it just went from good to bad to worse. I got everything from broken bones to skull fractures. I was hit with chainsaws. There were many beatings not bad enough to send me to the hospital, but when they were, he always drove me there. The hospital records prove that when my husband was home, I got hurt."

Becca was a strong, smart businesswoman who managed a crew of employees and earned more than $100,000 yearly running three farms. And yet, she said, "when it came to meeting Don one to one, I could not function. He brainwashed me so badly . . . I brainwashed myself so badly. I just felt trapped."

She didn't want to believe that she and her children were in terrible danger. She says, "If I had ever admitted to myself that he was capable of killing me, or one of my children, I wouldn't have been waiting for it to happen."

The escalating abuse, Becca observed, ran parallel to difficulties in the family. In the early eighties, Becca was told she had cancer and six months to live. Months of chemotherapy and several operations pushed the cancer into remission. Then their house burned down. Don's health started to deteriorate: his diabetes was causing his eyes to hemorrhage, and he began to take pills. Becca called them his "mean pills," because "he'd take one and go crazy all day."

Even though Becca wanted to believe that the fear of going blind and losing his $50,000-a-year truck-driving job brought on his abuse, she knew he'd also beaten his first wife, and terrorized her with the same gun that Becca later used to kill him.

"At the trial," Becca says, "they knew it was his gun because the same gun had entered a domestic quarrel twenty-some years earlier. He shot the house up with his other wife and children." But the prosecutor was able to convince the jury and the judge that Becca had intended to kill Don and carried the gun with her.

Becca says she never thought about killing Don, but she made a detailed plan to leave him. She even rented a house in another state. On the eve of departure, though, the kids pleaded with Becca to wait for their school report cards, which were due the next day. Don was out on the road, not expected back for a couple of days. Becca gave in to the children. "It's hard enough running, but seven kids at one time? Ninety-nine percent of women who stay in these violent situations do so because they have kids."

But Don returned unexpectedly. The next day, instead of heading for the state line as she had planned, Becca found herself struggling in the cab of Don's pickup after she told him that she and the children were leaving.

The trial lasted two weeks. The judge announced at the trial's opening that he didn't want to hear a word about abuse. And at the trial's end, he sent Becca to prison for life.

The cell block where Becca lives with several other women who also killed abusive men (along with those convicted for armed robbery, check forgery, and drug selling) is cluttered with family pictures,

Becca shot her husband in self-defense as he tried to choke her to death. Her sentence was life without parole for premeditated murder.

bibles, and holiday cards sent from home. If not for the patrolling male guards and the bars, the ward might be a college dormitory: the women huddled on their beds in nightgowns, eating popcorn, knitting, and watching TV. It's as if they've accepted a destiny they can't figure out how to change. "We believe God has a purpose for us being here," several lifers told me.

But any women's prison is an isolated and lonely place. Locked away for fifty years far from friends and family, Becca and other long-timers struggle constantly against despair. That's why Becca welcomed the letters she started receiving last year from Wayne, a Minnesota construction worker. He'd been drawn to Becca when he saw her on a television talk show filmed in the prison. They corresponded. He visited her. And in January 1991 they were married. They can't consummate their marriage because the prison, to prevent pregnancies, prohibits conjugal visits. But Wayne helps Becca keep her hopes alive. He's a lifeline to the world outside the walls, and her marriage is a signal that Becca is not resigned to life in prison.

Many of the long-timers fight back against the system that locked them up. In prison, Becca and Carol Klaus, another inmate who killed her ex-husband in self-defense, helped attorneys draft new legislation regarding battered women who kill. Passed by the state legislature in 1987, the law permits defendants in Missouri courts to testify about the battering they've endured and produce expert witnesses to explain to the jury the conditions a battered woman faces, and how she may be driven to defend herself. Since 1987, some women have appealed their convictions and won on the grounds that they were denied the help of expert testimony at their trials.

Becca also pushes for a new trial. "We aren't asking that the door open and turn us loose," Becca says, speaking for women locked up along with her, sentenced to life without parole for killing in self-defense. "We want a chance to get back in the courtroom and have what we haven't had yet—a fair, just trial."

In December 1990, Ohio Governor Richard Celeste released twenty-five battered women from his state prison who had been denied fair trials precisely because expert testimony about battering was excluded from the proceedings. Becca watched with jubilation. But her cell is in Missouri, and unless a similar miracle occurs there, she'll die in prison.

Only forty-one years old, Becca has survived two heart attacks. She is not able to do prison labor, but to keep up her health as well as her spirits, she regularly meets with other lifers to do aerobic exercises (above). Becca has been imprisoned since her arrest in 1984. Of her husband Don's abuse, she says, "For years I'd be asking him, 'Why did you do this to me?' He would say, 'You made me do it.'" Don also hit their five-year-old son Jamie. Striking her was one thing, Becca said, but going after the children was another. When Becca told Don she was leaving, she offered him half of everything she owned. He told her he didn't want half. "He said when I was dead, he would get it all," she recalls. That's when Don started choking Becca and she shot him. Becca kept the contact sheet of the police pictures used at her trial (left). They show his hands, which she scratched as she struggled for her life, a shattered window on the driver's side, a large man with dry bloodstains on his chest, and a brain lying on a stainless steel table in the county morgue. Becca said the police also took photos of her bruises. Those pictures disappeared before they could be shown in court. She hasn't given up hope that one day she'll get a retrial in which Don's history as a batterer will be admitted as evidence. "In my heart, I don't believe he is dead," she says, "because in all reality, he isn't. He still lives because we still live with what he did to us. Till we're dead, he won't be, because he was so bad."

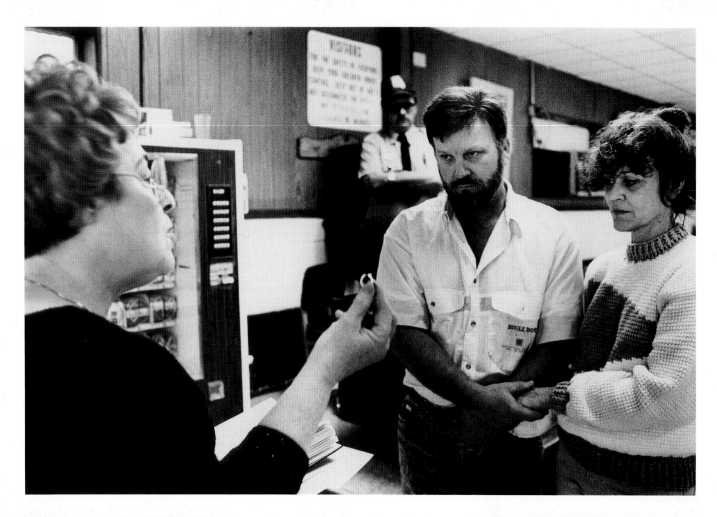

In the prison's snack bar (top), Becca married Wayne, a construction worker who'd fallen in love after seeing her on a TV talk show. Both believe that one day she will get out of prison, and until then, Wayne tries to keep Becca "in touch with the world outside."

I spent three days in a maximum-security prison for women in Jefferson City, Missouri, where it's estimated that seven out of ten women incarcerated were battered at some time in their lives.

Missouri is especially tough on women who kill. There are thirty-three women there sentenced to fifty years or life without parole for killing their abusive partners.

I arrived at the Renz Correctional Center on Christmas Day, 1990. At the entrance, the guards let me keep my cameras but took the car keys. The prisoners were amazed that I was actually planning to spend the night with them. They helpfully dug into their trunks to find gray polyester trousers for me, and sheets, a pillow, and a flowered comforter, which, they explained, would keep me from being eaten alive by the bedbugs in the mattress.

I was assigned to Dorm 9, where many of the long-timers live. Paint peels from the walls and large plastic sheets are draped about to catch rainwater that has been leaking for years through the ceiling above the beds and toilets. The bathrooms still have urinals from the days when this was a men's prison. The building has been condemned several times.

Prison is a kind of women's shelter, except that the women don't make the rules, and they can't leave.

Seventy women are squeezed together here, like ants in an underground kingdom, with orders to live in harmony. They're forbidden to show anger or hostility. They have no privacy and are told to expect no respect. The guards, mostly men, patrol the prisoners' bedsides and shower stalls. They pat search the women many times each day. The women's visits with their children are limited and nearly always monitored. Conjugal visits are not allowed. Any disobedience earns one or two weeks in "the hole."

At midnight, the main fluorescent light went out. I lay for hours, tossing on the sagging mattress and listening to the sounds: the rumbling fan that blew hot air across the room, the snoring, and the grinding of teeth. Just as I was falling asleep, an ugly, loud gong rang out. It was 4:30 a.m. and a guard shouted, "Morning wake-up!" as he walked along the rows of military-style bunk beds. The woman across from me, a forty-one-year-old mother of seven, sentenced to fifty years for killing her husband in self-defense, sprang from a bottom bunk. She dressed quickly in the dark, pulling on day clothes over long johns, brushed her hair, opened her trunk, took two mugs to the microwave, and

returned with tea and lozenges for me, because she'd heard me coughing through the night. She sipped her raspberry tea as she cross-stitched a child's quilt. These women were the most unlikely criminals.

Superintendent Bryan Goeke told me, "The long-timers tend to be relatively stable and adjust well. Especially if they ever want to have a chance to get out. Most of the battered women serving life-without-parole sentences in here are no problem. In fact, most of them are more socially well-adjusted than a large percent of my staff."

One guard observed, "When there were men here before, we had shotguns to keep them inside. The male drive, I guess, is wanting to get out and be free. The women are more used to having someone telling them what to do."

Verna Magers was twenty-eight when she was sentenced to twenty years here for killing her boyfriend. "I don't look at it as being murder," she said. "Lawrence was a six-foot-one-inch, 210-pound man. He had a black belt in karate. I'd known him for a year. I loved him. We were engaged, living in my mother's house. His personality turned on and off like a light switch. One minute he'd be smiling, the next minute my head would be slamming into a wall. At first he was like that just with me. Then he started getting worse, going to my children with it. That was it."

Verna confronted her boyfriend about undressing her eight-year-old daughter so he could spank her. "I looked him straight in the eye and asked him if he'd been sexually abusing my daughter. At first he got angrier and denied it. Then he said, 'Yeah. So what if I did? And I'll do it again if I feel like it.' He lay down on the sofa and looked up at the ceiling. I reached into my purse and pulled out a gun I carried for protection." (Verna had bought the gun after the last time the police responded to her call for protection from Lawrence's beatings: "Lady, unless we see it happen, we can't do anything about it.") "I fired two shots at his head. I'm not sorry for what I did. I wasn't going to let him get away with abusing my child again." While someone else cares for her two children, Verna will wait fifteen years for her parole review.

Most mothers have contemplated what they would do if anyone threatened their child's life. And the answer always seems to be: whatever is necessary. If a woman doesn't protect her children, or can't, society is swift to condemn her, just as so many people condemned Hedda Nussbaum. But when the bat-

Women who kill their husbands, even in self-defense, get very heavy sentences. Fifty years or even life without parole is common.

tered woman finds the strength to defend her children by killing an assailant, she is cast with serial killers and mass murderers. She loses her children and she is locked in prison for the better part of her life or, if the system has its way, till the day she dies.

Yet for the majority of long-timers in women's prisons, killing their abusive partner was their first criminal act. When women kill their abusers, it is almost invariably a last resort to protect themselves and their children from further harm. Superintendent Goeke told me, "We've got several women in this penitentiary for killing, and probably they had justification." Ironically, many battered women who plead guilty to murdering their husbands get shorter sentences than those who try to convince a judge and jury that they acted in self-defense.

"I think it is awfully hard for the public to understand what type of situations the women were living in," Goeke says. "The prosecutor's philosophy is always like this: 'Regardless of the situation she was living in, she had a choice. She should have gotten help; she should have done something different. Murder is not the way to solve the problem.' That sounds good and easy. But it's not always possible when she's got that individual telling her what he's going to do to her and the kids if she leaves. The fact

is, he's found her every time she's ever left. Then he beat her senseless and said, 'If you leave, I'm going to do it again.' It doesn't take long before she truly believes him, because he's done it time and time again. She is absolutely convinced in her own mind that regardless of what she does, he's going to get her and do what he promised. The track record in a lot of these situations has proven that."

Wandering one night among the wards in the Missouri prison, I overheard two women whispering through their cell bars.

Carol Williams: "If a man leans on you, you're supposed to take it, right?!"

Donna Ray Reed: "You're supposed to, because if you fight back . . ."

Carol Williams: "That's bullshit. If a man hits me, I'll fight back."

Donna Ray Reed: "Then you'll be doing thirty years like I'm doing. You're supposed to be able to say, 'Well, I'm going to leave.' But it's not always that easy or simple. There are always circumstances. I had money. I had a car. He always had a sad story. 'Oohhh, Donna, the heat's off in my apartment . . . can I come and stay with you.' And I always had a big heart. Now I wished I didn't have a heart at all . . ."

Justice is erratic. Carol Klaus (top), convicted of murder, is serving twenty-eight years for the death of her violent husband, a police officer. Belinda Keys (right) killed her husband in self-defense, pleaded guilty to murder, and was sentenced to six years. Verdia Miller (above) didn't kill anyone. One male friend planned to kill another, and threatened to kill Verdia if she told. Her silence made her an accomplice. She got fifty years to life in prison, while the killer himself got fifteen.

There is a quiet practicality about the "lifers" (seen on these pages) as they go about their daily routines inside the Renz maximum-security prison for women in Jefferson City. It underscores their ability to endure and survive. Their "crime" was self-preservation and these women appear

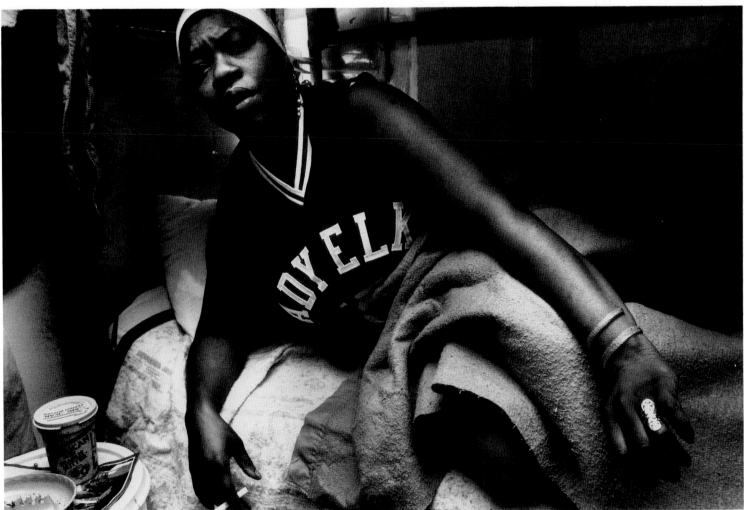

resigned—more like prisoners of war than violent criminals. Indeed, most have no previous convictions. They are ordinary people. Many are mothers and even grandmothers who've left children behind, although often it was the children they were trying to protect in the first place.

ACKNOWLEDGMENTS

This book owes everything to the courage of women and men who agreed to sacrifice some of their privacy in order to help others, so that the dark curtain that surrounds domestic violence could be pulled away. My deepest appreciation goes to the women in shelters and prisons for their trust, and for giving me the chance to know what they experienced in order to let the public learn from their stories.

Many people have made this book possible. My mother, Ann O'Malley Ferrato, strong and consistent, whose love kept Fanny safe during the long periods I was absent. Antoinette Pizzoferrato, who survived an abusive marriage, taught me the importance of listening to our grandmothers and mothers. Margie Soo Hoo Lee is the indisputable godmother of this book for her loving spirit, among the other good things she contributed. Renata Dualibi, Fanny's spiritual sister, and Lara Jealous, for dedication to the cause. Katherine Loving, who did the vital initial research. To the women in publishing who used their power to bring stories of domestic abuse out in mainstream magazines. My profound gratitude to Pat Ryan, former Managing Editor of *Life* magazine, and to Avery Rome, Managing Editor at *Philadelphia Inquirer Magazine*. To Carrie Tuhy, Karen Branan, Anne Hollister, Leslie Goldman, Julie Ades, Yukiko Launois, Grazia Neri, and Beth Filler. To Marty Friday, Susan Schechter, Dr. Lenore Walker, Sue Ostoff, Ellen Pence, Barbara Shaw, Esta Soler, Louise Bauschard, Caren Robinson, Joan Welch, Pat Kuta, Lisbeth Wolf, and Joan Sargent, for enriching me with their knowledge as longtime activists in the battered-women's movement. To Limor Inbar, the photography student who quickly became an integral member of this project and proved herself to be a magnificent printer. To Fumiko Yamato Fox, whose passion for photography still fills me with inspiration. To Leah Rhys, the headmistress who exhibited these photographs at my alma mater, Laurel School. To Lynne Honickman, for her commitment to sending this book across America to the people who are most in need. To Karen Emmons and Diana Stoll, for their resilience and heartfelt help with copy editing. To friends like Ruth Warren, Debbie Schorsch, Nina Rosenberg, Lisa Park, Lynn Goldsmith, Bea Armendariz, Reba Nichols, and Liz Detwiler for their multifaceted support throughout the book's evolution. To Ann Jones, for her invaluable collaboration as both sister and editor, making every day a revolutionary learning experience. Melissa Harris glided through the unenviable role as editor, peacemaker, marriage counselor, psychiatrist, and friend. Without Melissa this book would not have survived.

Standing next to these goddesses are the best men. My dad, P. J. Ferrato, a passionate photographer as well as a doctor, who deeply influenced me with his concern for humanity. Philip Jones Griffiths is the indisputable godfather of this book, because when everyone else said "Give it up!", Philip cried "Keep it up!" Philip has lived with and cared about every new chapter that I came home with over the last ten years. He alone could have designed it. Howard Chapnick brought his unwavering support, boyish energy, and irresistible charm to delivering the message of these photographs. Fred Ritchin took the project under his warm and protective wing from the very beginning, finding new ways to inform people with the pictures. Dick Stolley, with his desire to see women as winners, consistently came through with the most perceptive advice. Peter Howe, Director of Photography at *Life*, offered me the chance to show the problems of domestic violence anywhere in America, and he also

promised it would be published. Peter proved that his word was his honor. Mark Greenberg, of *Visions*, did much to support the project during early days and bravely faced down a killer snake—for the good of the book. Ross Baughman religiously sent me newspaper clippings about family violence. Snitzy Schneider kept his funnybone in the toughest times. Dereck Ashcroft helped me to create the Survivors of Domestic Abuse Association. Dick Polman, my true-blue partner on domestic-violence stories, has many times proven to be the most sensitive reporter alive. The rest of the team at the *Philadelphia Inquirer* who helped make the first publication of domestic-violence photographs in America such a rewarding experience were: Eugene Roberts, former Editor-in-Chief; Fred Mann, Editor; Larry Price, former Director of Photography; and David Griffin, former Art Director, who designed the magazine story across the walls at home while on his honeymoon! Special thanks to the following men for their efforts toward stopping the cycle of violence—Michael Lindsey, Michael Paymar, Fred Jealous, Hamish Sinclair, Barry Scheck, Bob Pledge, Superintendent Bryan Goeke, George Howe Colt, Ted Welch, Jim Hughes, Pedro Myer, Gordon Parks, Arnold Skolnik, Nigel Carr, Steve Shames, and Paul Curtis. Finally I thank Michael Hoffman, at Aperture. He was the first and only publisher who believed that *Living with the Enemy* was a photographic book that needed to be published.

Over the years certain organizations have been very supportive. The Women's Center and Shelter of Greater Pittsburgh, MAWS program for Women and Men in San Rafael, Boulder County Safehouse, Denver Safehouse, Women Against Abuse in Philadelphia, AWARE in Juneau, Women's Advocates in St. Paul, AMEND in Denver, Wilder Foundation (DAP) in Minnesota, Minnesota Intervention Project in Duluth, Men's Alternatives to Violence in Monterey. The McKeesport Police Department, the Philadelphia Police Department, the Minneapolis Police Department, the San Rafael Police Department. Women's Self-Help and WINN in St. Louis. National Clearinghouse for the Defense of Battered Women. Renz Correctional Center in Missouri. Shakopee Prison in Minnesota. Albert Einstein Emergency in Philadelphia, Hennipen Hospital in Minneapolis.

Thanks to the W. Eugene Smith Foundation, the Robert F. Kennedy Foundation, the Missouri School of Journalism, and to Eastman Kodak. To my agency, Black Star, and to everyone at Aperture, a heart full of appreciation.

If you wish to make a contribution toward ending violence in the home, contact Donna Ferrato, Domestic Assault Awareness Project, c/o Aperture, 20 East 23rd Street, New York, New York 10010.